THE BURREN &
THE ARAN ISLANDS
A WALKING GUIDE

TONY KIRBY, from Limerick, worked in Italy and Dublin before leaving the public sector in 2003 to start a new life in County Clare. He is now a full-time walking guide and heritage consultant based in the Burren. Tony lives in Caherblonick, near Killinaboy, with his wife and young sons.

Visit Tony's website at http://heartofburrenwalks.com
You can also stay up to date at:
  twitter.com/theburrenwalks
  www.facebook.com/pages/Heart-Burren-Walks/651987144816583

A variety of features on limestone caused by water erosion, Eimer Ní Riain.

Carran Loop - A hawthorn tree bent by the Atlantic wind.

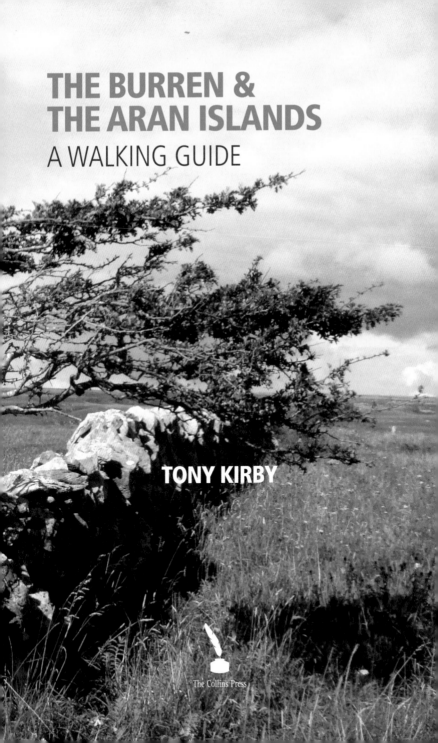

THE BURREN &
THE ARAN ISLANDS
A WALKING GUIDE

TONY KIRBY

The Collins Press

First published in 2014 by
The Collins Press
West Link Park
Doughcloyne
Wilton
Cork

Line illustrations courtesy of Carles Casasin
Photographs © Tony Kirby unless otherwise credited

A CIP record for this book is available from the British Library.

ISBN-13: 978-1-84889-200-2

Design and typesetting by Fairways Design
Typeset in Myriad Pro
Printed in Poland by Białostockie Zakłady Graficzne SA

Contents

A young trekker negotiates the crazy pavement

Introduction

The Burren and the Aran Islands can justly claim to be amongst the most distinctive landscapes in Europe. Limestone pavement is scarce and precious worldwide. However, it abounds in these two regions, which means they are places apart. Moreover, the juxtaposition of the limestone with the sea makes for some of the most dramatic coastal scenery in the west of Ireland.

The great essayist and writer Tim Robinson once poetically referred to the Burren's huge concentration of archaeological monuments as 'a vast memorial to bygone cultures'. The same could equally be said of the Aran Islands. The age-old practice of out-wintering cattle in the Burren uplands and the southern parts of the Aran Islands strikes a perfect harmony between man and nature. This low-intensity farming practice plays a critical role in transforming these specific areas each spring into a mosaic of beautiful wildflowers which originate from different climatic zones in the world.

These are just some of the reasons why the Burren and the Aran Islands make for some of the finest walking in these islands.

A group on a guided walk along one of the Burren's many green roads.

A variety of features on limestone caused by water erosion. Eimer Ní Riain

This book was written to help the walker to follow some of the best trails these regions have to offer. It was also written in the hope that it will assist in the reading of the rocky, majestic landscape.

Come and see, and may you never tire of the trails.

Go n-éirí an bóthar leat.

The Walks

Although abilities vary greatly amongst walkers, I have divided the walks into three grades to help the reader to select the walks best suited to his/her ability.

Casual signifies mostly even gradient and smooth terrain. Short distances.
Moderate represents some ascent/descent and some rough terrain. Reasonable distances.
Strenuous means hillwalking and rough terrain. Reasonable distances.

The times for each walk have been calculated on the basis of 1.6km (1 mile) per hour approximately for the strenuous walks and 3.2km (2 miles) per hour approximately otherwise.

Maps

Ordnance Survey of Ireland (OSI) *Discovery Series* (www.osi.ie) or *Folding Landscape* (www.foldinglandscapes.com) as outlined in the walk descriptions are recommended. *The Folding Landscape* series provides excellent detail on the built heritage.

Chronology

Stone Age 4000–2000 BC
Bronze Age 2000–600 BC
Iron Age 600 BC –AD 400
Early Christian AD 400–800 (also part of Early Medieval period)
Medieval AD 800–1500

Safety

An awareness of the risks that trekking can present is the key to planning for any eventuality. Weather, and topographical and human hazards can combine in any number of scenarios, the outcome of which will greatly depend on training, experience and preparation. The variety in Irish terrain and conditions makes a definitive list of dos and don'ts for the uplands impossible; the following, however, should always be considered before you make that first step into the hills:

- Be realistically adventurous, bearing in mind your current ability, fitness and experience.
- Learn to interpret the national and regional weather forecasts for the hill environment, but always take heed of local conditions.
- Learn to navigate without dependency on technology, marked trails or other users.
- Equip yourself realistically for your planned journey, taking into account weather, terrain and duration.
- Wear sturdy, comfortable walking boots and waterproof clothing. At a minimum, bring map, compass, water, food, first-aid kit and mobile phone. Please remember that mobile phone coverage can be uneven, particularly in the uplands.
- Carry emergency back-up equipment for the unexpected, but do not overburden yourself.
- Acknowledge and consider your actions on other users of the uplands.
- Never push on regardless: if unsure, be safe and return another day.
- The Mountaineering Council of Ireland runs excellent safety and training programmes. www.mci.ie

The Burren Code

The Burren Code is an inter-agency joint initiative designed to inform people regarding appropriate behaviour when visiting the region. Please support the code and help protect the region's rich natural and cultural heritage.

- Leave limestone pavement as you find it
- Preserve natural habitats and leave wildflowers undisturbed
- Take care not to damage monuments, walls or buildings
- Respect landowners, their property and their livestock
- Park and camp in designated areas

Leave No Trace

Leave No Trace is an Outdoor Ethics Programme that promotes responsible outdoor recreation through education, research, and partnerships. Please follow the principles of Leave No Trace:

- Plan ahead and prepare
- Be considerate of others
- Respect farm animals and wildlife
- Travel and camp on durable ground
- Leave what you find
- Dispose of waste properly
- Minimise the effects of fire

For more information please visit www.leavenotraceireland.org

Useful Websites

www.burren.ie The Burren Eco Tourism Network. Eco tourism providers in the Burren promoting responsible travel.

www.burrenbeo.ie The Burrenbeo Trust Limited is an inclusive, membership-based organisation dedicated to the conservation of the Burren.

www.burrengeopark.ie The Burren Cliffs of Moher Geopark. A Geopark is a unified area with geological heritage of international significance.

www.burrenlife.ie Now named Burren Farming for Conservation Programme. Ireland's first major Farming for Conservation programme.

www.burrennationalpark.ie A National Parks & Wildlife Service (NPWS) website giving detailed information regarding heritage and conservation in the National Park. It also details the Park's walking trails.

www.clarebirdwatching.com The superb website of the Clare branch of BirdWatch Ireland.

www.discoverireland.ie/campaigns/shannon-walking-trails Fáilte Ireland website which includes trails and maps for the Burren region.

www.foldinglandscapes.com Quality map series provides excellent detail on the built heritage.

www.heartofburrenwalks.com Heart of Burren Walks offers a wide range of guided walks led by the author.

www.mci.ie The Mountaineering Council of Ireland runs excellent safety and training programmes.

www.osi.ie The Ordnance Survey of Ireland (OSI) *Discovery Series* of maps recommended for walking in the Burren.

Slievecarran Loop

*'We must reconcile ourselves to the stones,
not the stones to us.'*
Hugh MacDiarmid, 'On A Raised Beach' (1934)

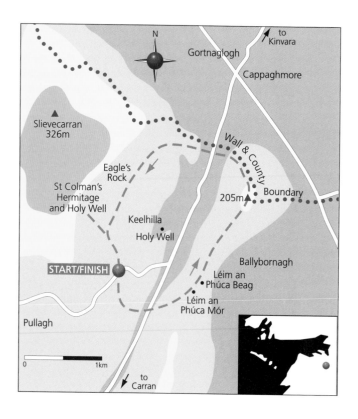

Start/finish: From Kinvarra on N67 heading towards Ballyvaughan, take the first turn left about 1km from the village. You soon come to a 'Y' in the road. Take the left option. Proceed to a four-cross road. Drive straight through, then take the next turn right. Continue for over a kilometre till you reach the Slieve Carran Nature Reserve entrance on the right-hand side of the road. Parking is available here.

Description: A challenging hill walk with uneven terrain. Some steep ascents and descents.

Highlights: A nature reserve with a wide floral range; an Early Christian hermitage with holy well; fine vistas of the east of the Burren and the legend of Bóthar na Miasa.

Distance: 8km (5 miles)

Time: 4.5 hours

Grade: Strenuous

Map: *The Burren – a map of the uplands of northwest Clare*. Folding Landscapes. Scale: 1:31,680 or OSI *Discovery Series* Map No. 52. Scale: 1:50,000.

The walk takes place in the Burren National Park. The park is approximately 1,500 hectares in area and is located in the southeast of the region. It is managed by the NPWS for nature conservation and public access. It is one of six National Parks in the Republic of Ireland.
(1) Pass through the stile across the road from the Nature Reserve entrance and follow the yellow trail markers. You have entered a of 45-hectare mosaic of limestone

Burnet rose. Its rosehips are rich in vitamin C.
Ciarán Ó Riain

pavement and grasslands which is farmed through the Burren Farming for Conservation Programme (BFCP, formerly Burren Life programme). The programme is based in Carran village and is Ireland's first major farming for conservation initiative. In 2013, over €1.114m was allocated to Burren farmers through BFCP by the Department of Agriculture and the farmers co-funded over 1,250 separate tasks in the 160 participating farms in order to improve the biodiversity of each farm. Tasks included removal of scrub, protection of water sources, repair of stone walls and restoration of damaged habitats. Cattle graze this particular area in winter as part of the programme. The effect of the winter grazing of these uplands (reverse transhumance) is quite spectacular in spring as the area is transformed into a wildflower-rich habitat.

(2) Proceed along a worn path in a southerly direction until you reach a drystone wall. Walk alongside the wall heading due east. Dropwort blooms here from May to September. A relative of meadowsweet, though its flowers are unscented, its distribution in Ireland is very limited. In fact, it can only be found in the east of the Burren, east Clare and southeast Galway.

(3) The trail changes from worn path to an old unsurfaced road. The road was built about 150 years ago in order to link two minor roads. The hill range in the background is Turloughmore. You will see two distinct depressions at the summit – Léim an Phúca Mór (Big Fairy Leap) and Léim an Phúca Beag (Small Fairy Leap). There is copious scrub on either side of the trail. You may notice a drystone wall on your left. This would suggest that the area was used for rough grazing for livestock in the past. Once the land was abandoned, the inevitable ecological succession was the scrub.

(4) The scrub is primarily hazel. However, you will pass under a spindle tree which arches across the trail. The lime-loving spindle is usually no more than a shrubby tree but this particular specimen has reached lofty heights. The pink fruits are quite a spectacle in autumn; although poisonous to humans and livestock, the fruit can be safely eaten by birds. A few holly trees intersperse the hazel scrub. The fruit of the holly, borne only by the female tree, is not very nice to taste but it is harmless. An occasional ash tree may also be seen towering over the scrub. This is the start of the climax vegetation as the Burren uplands progressively cedes to hazel–ash woodland with the decline of the ancient transhumance tradition.

(5) You emerge from scrub to grasslands. At this point, leave the yellow trail by going though a gate below you. Cross the minor road and go through another gate which leads up a track. You will soon pass by a small building and ascend the slopes of Turloughmore, going northeastwards.

(6) The walk changes direction now from northeast to north as you begin walking right alongside the wall for 2km. When you have advanced 200m, descend slowly and carefully across a limestone ledge onto a pavement area. It may appear barren; however, as you walk across it, you will notice a number of different tree species growing in the grikes (fissures) including hazel, holly and hawthorn. The trees are growing at bonsai levels for two reasons: firstly, because of the shallowness of the soil in which they are rooted; secondly, to avoid the depredations of the wind in the open expanse.

The presence of wildflowers and trees in the apparently barren pavement habitat prove that the Burren has well earned its moniker of 'The Fertile Rock'.

There are silver birch several metres high on the other side of the wall where there is more soil and shelter. Birch can tolerate higher ground better than other native trees.

(7) A drystone wall intersects the 2km-long wall. Climb over it to resume walking along the course (north) of the wall and enter into a grasslands area. Take great care always when crossing drystone walls. If you dislodge any stones, please put them back in their original positions. You will see what appears to be an unfinished drystone wall on the left. It is in fact a livestock shelter. The wall was built along a north–south axis as the prevailing winds in Ireland are southwesterly. Note also the heavy concentration of dung on the eastern (leeward) side of the shelter wall.

You are now climbing to the most northerly peak in the Turloughmore range, 205m above sea level. Look over the wall as you progress and you will see the ruins of drystone walls looking like tipped dominoes. They are known as slab walls and have been dated to Early Christian times. These walls were believed to act as field boundaries on the land associated with ring forts. You may have the good luck to see the mountain hare in the uplands. It is often seen in open habitats and feeds on a mixture of plant material including heather.

(8) You arrive at the summit. There are a pair of small stone hilltop markers here. This peak is the most easterly on the Turloughmore range.

Slievecarran is to the west and the pasture and silage grasslands to the east are located between Kinvarra (north) and Gort (east). There are almost ninety different breeding bird species in the Burren National Park in part because of the variety of habitats which the park has to offer. However, the number of species breeding on limestone plateaus such as this with its cliffs, ledges and limestone pavement is quite limited. The wheatear is one bird which favours open ground like this. It has a distinctive white rump and flicks its tail and wings frequently.

Make your descent along the wall which now veers left (west) and downwards along the slopes

The wheatear is a chat which breeds both in the Burren and on the Aran Islands

9

to a road which is effectively a mountain pass between Turloughmore and Slievecarran. The wall is in excellent condition and was probably built during the last great wall-building programme in the region, in the eighteenth and nineteenth centuries. The walls were built to remove stone from the land to improve it, to provide some shelter for livestock from the elements and also to define field and property boundaries.

You pass through a small, waterlogged area where rush is the dominant plant. Such a waterlogged area in an otherwise free-draining limestone expanse is unusual. You pass under telegraph wires, walk through a thicket and climb over a wall before you cross the road. When you enter the field at the other side of the road, you are faced with a sudden sharp ascent over three cliffs in order to reach a terrace on the slopes of Slievecarran. You are heading west. The second cliff is reached by passing through some light hazel scrub whilst the third cliff involves walking through some scrub and pavement.

Once you have negotiated these cliffs, you reach an extensive terrace and you will see a long drystone wall running along the base of the slopes of Slievecarran straight ahead of you to the west. Make your way to the wall, turning left just before it and start walking southwards for

about 1km, following the course of the wall. You will eventually reach the path for St Colman Mac Duagh's hermitage.

Feral goats are frequently spotted in this immediate area. The goat was one of the earliest animals to be domesticated and was probably introduced to Ireland from the Bay of Biscay area 3,000

The holy well at St Colman Mac Duagh's hermitage.

to 4,000 years ago. Some goats have not resigned themselves to the domestic condition and have been making their way back out into the wild. Their role as landscape managers in arresting the advance of hazel scrub has been overstated by some: scientific evidence now suggests that hazel is not high up on the menu of the Burren goats.

(9) When you have walked about a kilometre along the drystone wall under the slopes of Slievecarran, you will see a T-shaped livestock shelter on your left. The ingenious T-shape of the wall guarantees the livestock shelter no matter what the direction of the wind and rain. You will also see a decayed wall to the right of the stock shelter.

Make your way through this wall and walk along for a short distance until you reach an impressive area of what looks like polished limestone

Clints and grikes. The clints are blocks; the grikes are fissures. Eimer Ní Riain

pavement. There is a small drystone construction known as a turf tile in the middle of the pavement area. These structures were used to dry domestic fuel such as turf or 'cockbow' (cow dung).

Rainwater solution has widened the grikes between the limestone blocks, or clints, over the millennia, and has carved out beautiful forms on the pavement by chemically dissolving the limestone, some of which look like footprints and horses' hooves. Legend has it that St Colman Mac Duagh's manservant expressed a desire to eat meat after a period of strict Lenten observance in the nearby hermitage. Colman took pity on the servant and prayed on his behalf. At that moment the king's Easter feast was taking place in Dunguaire Castle in nearby Kinvarra. The dishes in the castle suddenly took flight and made their way to the hermitage, with the king and his men in hot pursuit. Colman started praying again, whereupon the feet of the king's men and the horses' hooves got stuck in the pavement. The pavement area is known as Bóthar na Miasa (the road of the dishes). The legend is an original and imaginative explanation of these curious karst features.

(10) Bóthar na Miasa is bordered by a drystone wall. Walk southwards alongside the wall until you meet a worn path. A gate with a stile is to your left but you turn right along the path to reach St Colman's Hermitage. The hermitage is secluded at the end of the path in mature ash and hazel woodland at the base of Eagle's Rock. Colman's choice of an ascetic existence in this isolated location was part of the tradition in the early centuries of Christendom in Ireland. He lived in the sixth century, so his original oratory was undoubtedly made of wood. The base of the oratory at the site now consists of large irregular blocks in a building tradition known as cyclopean, which may date from the eleventh century. The oratory is a ruin now and is in danger of being further degraded by the advance of hazel within it. Colman's *leaba* or bed is said to have been in the cave

11

A votive offering and hart's-tongue fern at St Colman's Well, Eagle's Rock.

just above the oratory. There are two leachtanna (stone altars) at the site and a holy well. The well water is said to cure backache. Some people still frequent the well out of spiritual conviction.

The site is set in a mature hazel woodland with a floor rich in ferns, mosses and liverworts. It brings to mind a tropical rainforest. The white flower of the ramsons, our only native garlic, enhances the beauty of the hermitage in spring.

(11) Make your way to the start/finish at the nature reserve entrance by walking back along the oratory path.

Some of the flora species you may see here as you walk the last few hundred metres of the loop are carline thistle, mountain avens, spring gentian, Irish eyebright and the fly orchid. Carline thistle is part of the Mediterranean range of flora, mountain avens is Arctic and the gentian is Alpine.

There is a small range of fifteen flora species native to Ireland, which are largely absent from Great Britain. They are wildflowers with origins in northern Spain and Portugal. Irish eyebright is one of these and it can be seen here in spring. Its distribution in Ireland and Britain is quite thin, confined as it is to a small number of stations in the west of Ireland.

The fly orchid uses its scent to attract flies and bees. Male flies are attracted to the fragrance and attempt to mate with the orchid, thereby effecting cross-pollination when they visit a series of flowers on different plants.

(12) You have now completed the loop and have returned to the start/finish point at the nature reserve entrance gates. A final thought is that the Burren is very slowly disappearing due to its dissolution by rainwater. In fact, the Burren uplands will have totally disappeared in 2 to 3 million years and the land surface will be at sea level all the way from Galway Bay in the west of the Burren to the Gort lowlands in east Galway. As you treat yourself to a last glance at the slopes of Slievecarran and the hilltops of Turloughmore, you may console yourself with the thought that you have made the most of them before they vanish.

Carran Loop

'… feel the pulse of this perfumed earth, and the heartbeat of these ancient stones.'
P. J. Curtis, 'The Sound of Stone' (2003)

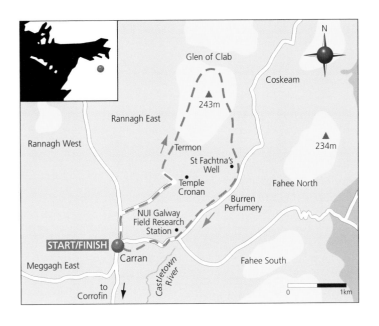

Start/finish: Carran village. From Corrofin, follow the R476, heading towards Kilfenora/Lisdoonvarna. When you reach Leamaneh Castle junction, turn right onto the R480 going in the direction of Ballyvaughan. Drive along the R480 for 1.5km until you come to a junction with a signpost for Carran. Turn right here as indicated and drive straight on for 5.5km until you reach the village of Carran. Cassidy's Pub is the prominent building on the right-hand side of the road as you enter the village.

Description: A challenging but invigorating walk in the Burren uplands. The trail is waymarked. Much of the terrain is uneven. The walk includes an ascent and descent of the slopes of Termon Hill (243m).

Highlights: An Early Christian site, two holy wells, a huge array of wildflowers and great vistas of parts of Counties Galway and Clare.

Distance: 9km (5.5 miles)

Time: 4.5 hours

Grade: Strenuous

Map: *The Burren – a map of the uplands of northwest Clare.* Folding Landscapes. Scale: 1:31,680 or OSI *Discovery Series* Map No. 51. Scale: 1:50,000.

(1) With Cassidy's pub at your back, turn right and walk down the village street. The old stone schoolhouse (built in 1858) is on your right at the bottom of the street. A small plaque above the door states that Michael Cusack once taught in this school. Born in the parish of Carran, Cusack was one of the founders of the Gaelic Athletic Association and was also the inspiration for the heavily lampooned fictional character 'The Citizen' in James Joyce's *Ulysses*. The former school building is currently home to the Burren Life Project, Ireland's first major farming-for-conservation project.

(2) Continue straight on for 500m, then turn right down a minor surfaced road. Walk 1km to the end of this road where there is a stile alongside a metal gate. Cross over the stile.

The magnificent Early Christian site of Termon (from Irish, meaning 'church land affording sanctuary') is in a field to your right. The site includes a single-celled chapel with human and animal heads. The chapel is dedicated to St Cronan. There is a tomb-shrine in the churchyard, which houses the bones of saints. These shrines were the object of much veneration by pilgrims in medieval times. There is also a holy well at the

A sheep's pass in a drystone wall, one of many vernacular structures to be found on Burren farms.

base of a very low cliff in the field to the east of the church, the waters of which are said to provide a cure for sore eyes.

(3) On climbing over the stile turn sharply left where a 30m-long animal track will bring you to another metal gate. Climb the stile on the left of the gate, turn right and begin climbing a tractor trail.

There is a large expanse of scrub to the north. Blackbirds, wrens and robins are just some of the bird species which abound in this habitat. Hazel is by far the most prolific tree species in the Burren scrub but blackthorn and whitethorn are part of the mosaic as well.

The scientific coordinator of the Burren Life Project, Dr Sharon Parr, has mapped the Burren habitats. She has concluded that 14 per cent of the Burren uplands have been colonised by scrub and that a further 5 to 10 per cent are scrub-affected. Rank grasses and dead plants accumulate in areas of the uplands where winter grazing by beef cattle

St Cronan's holy well, Carran.

15

has been reduced. Cattle grazing the hills in the winter months prevent the build-up of rank vegetation and suppress the growth of scrub. The cattle are, in effect, fulfilling a critical ecological role in protecting the most important flower habitats of the region: limestone pavement, orchid-rich grasslands and wetlands.

(4) You will come to a fork in the tractor trail. Looking south/southeast, you will see a white building: this is the field research station of the National University of Ireland Galway (opened in 1975). It provides facilities for research personnel from the university and visiting parties are also welcome. The Burren's largest turlough, the Carran turlough, is just beyond the research station to the east of Cassidy's pub. Slievecallan (391m) is the most prominent hill to the southeast and is situated in mid-Clare. Long before the advent of Met Éireann, the forecast in Carran was relayed by a goat farmer who could foretell the weather thanks to his scrutiny of Slievecallan from his vantage point in these hills. The area immediately around you is host to an array of orchids in spring and summer, including the early-purple orchid, pyramidal orchid, fragrant orchid and common spotted-orchid. Take the left turn at the fork as indicated by the marker.

(5) At the next junction you again opt for a left turn. The remains of the drystone wall to the left of the track consist of large, overlapping flags of limestone. These are known as slab walls and are the boundary walls of the field systems of protected farmsteads (ring forts) dating from the Early Christian period.

(6) You next come to a sharp elbow. Turn right here and walk parallel to a long drystone wall on your left. Orchid-rich grasslands lie to your left as you progress. The Burren is home to one-sixth of Ireland's total of such grasslands. The

Early-purple orchid – a common spring flower in the Burren and Aran Islands. Emma Glanville

industrialisation of farming has caused the demise of this important habitat in most of the rest of the country. However, the seasonal grazing of the uplands in this region strikes a perfect balance between man and

A hawthorn tree bent by the Atlantic wind.

nature and protects this habitat. Perpetuating this low-intensity farming is key to maintaining the huge wealth of natural heritage in the Burren hills.

(7) The loop is waymarked with over fifty limestone slabs, which have been placed in fissures in the rocks. Each slab contains a disc with a silver-coloured arrow and the words 'National Looped Walk'. There is one located about 400m on from the sharp elbow and 25m before a metal gate. Go left as indicated by the arrow. You are now trekking due north towards a valley known as Clab (from Irish, meaning 'open mouth'), along a shoulder of Termon Hill.

(8) As you progress, walk parallel to a very long drystone wall to your left. Go slightly right just after a wind-blown hawthorn and climb through a stile in the wall. Keep left along the drystone wall until you come to the corner of the field. Large field systems with improved grasslands are to be seen to the west across the valley. The next upright clint serves as an excellent viewing point of the limestone hills of Cappanawalla and Gleninagh off to the northwest. The two hills form a perfect frame for the highlands of Connemara even further to the northwest across Galway Bay.

(9) The next marker is another tall, erect clint located 40m beyond the upright marker at (8) above. Stroll 120m from this marker to a decayed drystone wall with two great vertical stones in it. A collapsed *caiseal* (ring fort/fortified farmstead) is just to the right. There are approximately 450 ring forts in the region. The social environment of the forts was family-based, hierarchical and inegalitarian.

Go over the wall and veer slightly right as indicated by the next marker. Some of the highest points in the Burren are to be found in the Poulacapple shale ridge off to the west (left). The ridge is easy to pick out as it is home to great stands of commercial forestry and telecommunications antennae. Go though a stile in the next wall. Keep an eye out for a lintelled gap in the drystone wall left of the stile. The gap allows sheep to pass through the wall from one grazing area to another. Walk parallel to this drystone wall. Galway Bay can be glimpsed to the north. Continue northwards, keeping the drystone wall on your left.

(10) You will pass four more markers along the next kilometre of the trail. The fourth marker is an upright only half a metre in height. Its arrow indicates a sharp right at this point and a change in the direction of the walk from north to east. You now go over a small crest to the next marker on a broad, low stone a mere 100m further on. The impressive valley to your left, the Glen of Clab, was formed by the collapse of cave passages. The woods in the glen provide dense cover and a lot of forage, in the form of berries, for badgers and pine martens. Gortaclare Mountain (290m) lies just beyond the glen to the north.

One of the largest terrestrial wind farms in Europe is located on the Old Red Sandstone of the Slieve Aughty range in east Galway, many kilometres straight ahead.

(11) There are three markers in the next 90m. The third marker is located at a stile in a drystone wall. Go through the stile. Walk into a small depression in the centre of this field where you will find your next marker. Honeysuckle can be quite plentiful in this area. Even though it is most commonly associated with woods, scrub and hedgerows, honeysuckle occasionally grows in the grikes between the limestone pavements where woodland conditions prevail. The parasitic thyme broomrape is also in evidence hereabouts. It draws sap from its host plant, wild thyme. Look southwards from this point and you will see three tall limestone uprights with markers.

(12) On reaching the third upright, turn left as indicated by the marker and start your descent from Termon Hill. Your next major landmark will be the holy well of Saint Fachtna, which is near the road, approximately 1km southeast from this point. Whilst the road is not visible at this juncture, you can clearly see the telegraph wires running along it. There are about a dozen markers between you and the well.

(13) Descend parallel to the drystone wall on your right for about 600m. You then reach a marker between clumps of hazel, which indicates a right turn through the same wall. On passing through this wall, descend 30m in the direction of the road as indicated by the next marker. You again turn right and walk parallel to the road. You are once more walking parallel to a drystone wall. Walk alongside until you find a gap as indicated by the marker. Go though the gap and follow the markers until you reach the well.

(14) Holy wells have pagan origins yet are venerated to this day for

their supernatural healing properties. The altar in this case is a drystone construction above the well itself.

The votive offerings include exotically coloured stones, seashells and coins. Christianity has been trying for almost 2,000 years to adopt these pagan monuments as its own. The well water in this case is also believed to be a remedy for sore eyes. The drystone constructions about 30m west of the well are penitential stations. Many people visit sacred wells to seek pardon for wrongdoing. The faithful walk around the stations a specific number of times, praying in a mantra-like fashion. The Aran Islands are the only other region in Ireland where these curious monuments still survive.

(15) The next leg of the trek is from the holy well to the NUI Galway Research Station – a distance of 1.75km. Stay on the side of the road where the well is situated. Walk southwestwards, keeping parallel to the road. The trail is waymarked clearly with a marker on average every 100m. The slopes of Fahee North to the east are distinguished by vertical bands of grass-covered boulder clay (an amalgam of rock, soil and clay debris deposited by glaciers during the Ice Age).

(16) The next marker is located in a wet meadow. Such a habitat is quite rare in the well-drained limestone expanse of the Burren. Hazel is prolific all around the meadow, although it cannot take hold in the meadow itself on account of the poor drainage. Continue in a southwesterly direction to a wall. Go through a stile and stroll through some hazel scrub for 120m to reach the next marker. Cassidy's public house is on the hill ahead slightly to the right of the marker. The end is now in sight. The third marker after this serves as a vantage point for the Fahee turlough to the east across the road. Ireland's oldest working perfumery, The Burren Perfumery, is set in secluded woodland beside the turlough and is home also to an excellent organic cafe.

(17) Continue southwestwards for another kilometre, indicated by six successive markers. At the sixth marker, take a sharp left and descend in the direction of the road.

Walk under the telegraph wires and turn right just after a water station for cattle, which you will find on your right, heading towards a bungalow 100m away. Go through a stile in the wall just beyond the bungalow. This will bring you onto a lay-by. Turn right here and walk along the surfaced road. You pass by the NUI research station on the right-hand side. Turn left into the first laneway after the station and walk along it for 100m as indicated by the marker. Turn right then and trek the short distance up to the village street. When you arrive at the street turn left and walk the final 100m to the start/finish point at Cassidy's pub.

(18) The pub serves good food and drink in high season and affords excellent views of the Carran polje.. The word 'polje' comes from Serbo-Croat and signifies a flat-floored depression hollowed out in the rock by rainwater erosion. Poljes are characterised by steep, enclosing flanks. The

7km^2 floor of the Carran polje is covered with glacial sediment, making for fertile land. The pasture is highly regarded, even though cattle can only graze it on a seasonal basis. Some of the flanks of the polje have vertical bands of boulder clay running down them.

Swallow holes in the polje floor drain away surface water into the underground water channels. However, these channels are unable to draw down all surface water in periods of high rainfall. Thus a temporary lake or turlough is formed on the surface. When the turlough waters disappear underground they wash the grasslands with calcium. The bone structure of the cattle is enhanced by eating these calcium-rich grasses. The Carran turlough in full flood covers 1.5km^2 of the polje floor and is the largest turlough in the region.

Famine Relief Road & Mullaghmore Red Trail

'Where they died, there the road ended
And ends still.'
Eavan Boland, 'That the Science of Cartography is Limited' (1994)

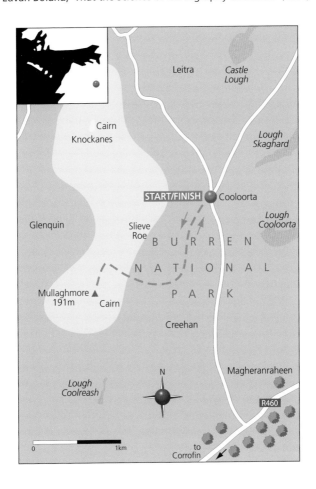

Start/finish: Follow the R460 from Corrofin to Gort. Take the third turn left which is located 9km along the route. Continue for 3km along this minor road until you reach a junction. The start point is at the gate and stile on the left-hand side of the road.

Description: An energetic walk to the summit of Mullaghmore (191m) with descent by the same outward route. Much of the terrain is uneven. The trail is waymarked with red-coloured markers.

Highlights: A nineteenth-century Famine relief road, a kid goat's stone pen, a drumlin, fine views of parts of counties Clare and Galway, a prehistoric hilltop cairn and a very rich and varied range of Burren flora in spring and summer.

Distance: 8km (5 miles)

Time: 3.5 hours

Grade: Strenuous

Map: *The Burren – a map of the uplands of northwest Clare.* Folding Landscapes. Scale: 1:31,680 or OSI *Discovery Series* Map No. 52. Scale: 1:50,000.

Author's Note: The walk takes place in the Burren National Park. The park is approximately 1,500 hectares in area and is located in the southeast of the region. It is managed by the NPWS for nature conservation and public access. It is one of six National Parks in the Republic of Ireland.

(1) Pass through the stile beside the metal gate at the lay-by to reach the start of the walk. The first part of the walk consists of an unsurfaced road. You will reach a red marker at the 200m mark indicating a right-hand turn onto the limestone pavement. However, you continue straight on along the unsurfaced road to make a short but very interesting diversion from the waymarked trail. You will rejoin the trail at a prominent drumlin (a low whale-back-shaped mound consisting of compacted boulder clay shaped by past glacial action) on the right of the road less than a kilometre from here.

The unsurfaced road is known as a Famine relief road and was built in the 1840s by local peasants. The historical context is the last great Irish potato famine, known also as The Great Hunger. Blight caused the failure of the potato crop for six successive years, from 1845–50. As the potato was the sole food of 3 million peasants in the west of Ireland, the consequences were catastrophic. Out of a population of 8 million people, approximately 1 million died and over a million emigrated. The government launched a scheme of public works in 1846 in order to deal with the crisis. However, the scheme was an abject failure for several reasons and was abandoned altogether in 1847. This unfinished road was built as part of that scheme.

Feral kid goats in the Burren National Park.
Stefan Wuertz

(2) Slieve Roe (188m) is the hill to your right (west). Red valerian lends great colour to this initial section of the unsurfaced road in spring, with its dark pink flowers. The road is bordered at either side by limestone pavement. Bloody crane's-bill, yellow-wort and rue-leaved saxifrage all prosper on the pavement in spring. Bloody crane's-bill is a showy geranium with bright red-purple flowers. Yellow-wort is distinguished by its boat-shaped leaves. It is known as *dréimire buí* in Irish – the yellow ladder. Rue-leaved saxifrage is an early spring flower. Dr Caleb Threlkeld, who published the first book on the flora of Ireland in the eighteenth century, was convinced that this saxifrage could cure a form of tuberculosis known as scrofula and advised: 'Take an handful of it. Boil it every morning in a quart of small beer. Strain it and drink it for your ordinary drink for a long time.'

(3) You will see a long, flat limestone rock about 25m to the right of the road at the 800m mark. It is splashed with a white lichen. When you walk 100m beyond this point, you will see that the relief road bisects a depression containing species-rich grasslands. This area abounds with primroses and cowslips in spring. The grasslands are quite conspicuous as they are surrounded by a great limestone expanse. If you look to the right (west), you will see the drumlin above you. You can also see a very long drystone wall and cliffs beyond the drumlin on the slopes of Mullaghmore. Leave the Famine relief road and begin the gentle climb across uneven terrain to the drumlin. As you progress, it is worth looking back for a moment to see the large regular blocks that buttress the flank of the relief road. The flank of the road is up to 4m in height and the labour involved must have been very arduous given that the workforce was starving.

(4) You will come to a small drystone enclosure about halfway between the road and the drumlin. It is known as a *cró* (meaning pen or enclosure). There are still several hundred such pens scattered across the Burren uplands, which indicate that goat farming was widespread in the region in the past.

Most are believed to date from the nineteenth century. The kid goat was kept in the stone-built pen by day and was thus restricted to a diet of its mother's milk. The meat from such a kid was tenderer than that from a grass-fed kid. Kid goat meat was a typical dish in the Burren in the past.

The Burren is renowned for its cultural heritage of tombs, castles and forts. However, the region's uplands are also littered with a myriad of fascinating vernacular monument types such as kid goats' pens, turf tiles (stone structures for drying fuel), sheeps' passes (gaps in walls to facilitate sheep movements), livestock shelters, herdsmen's cottages and drystone walls. Only a small amount of research has been conducted to date into this aspect of the Burren's built landscape. One of Ireland's most respected archaeologists, Dr Peter Harbison, has said that we 'concentrate too often on the better-known monuments at the expense of the less-striking examples, which tend to be overlooked. Without a knowledge of all of them our picture of the Burren would have to remain less than complete.'

(5) Walk from the pen towards the drumlin. When you reach the base of the drumlin cross over the ruins of a drystone wall and start the gentle climb to the top of the drumlin. The drumlin is favoured by out-wintering cattle on account of its lush grasslands. The upland pasture does not get waterlogged due to the excellent drainage afforded by the thin soils and limestone pavement. The drumlin's species-rich grasslands are calcium-rich and free-draining.

The grasslands host a wide range of wildflowers thanks to the low-intensity seasonal grazing. Late summer flowers here include yellow-rattle and devil's-bit scabious. Yellow-rattle can produce some of its own nutrients by photosynthesis but it is a hemiparasitic plant as it draws some water and nutrients from its host plant. Devil's-bit scabious has a mass of purple flowers on a wiry stem and is an important food source for insects and butterflies.

The Burren is home to thirty of Ireland's thirty-two butterfly species. The diversity of butterflies in the region is due to the plentiful food supply afforded by the rich range of flora. The brimstone is one of the heralds of spring in the region. The male's bright yellow colour is very striking.

(6) From the top of the drumlin, start walking down its western slope. When you reach the bottom, you will see a red marker on a vertical limestone rock on a ridge above you. Cross the wall and climb up to the low ridge to the marker. You have now rejoined the red waymarked trail.

(7) Continue to the next marker, which is a short distance further to the right. You are now walking along a worn cattle path that has been stone-bordered recently. You will see an erratic on the right of the path as you climb. You can also see a cliff face above you at the top of the path. When you reach the cliff face, climb it and turn left as indicated. It is only 10m to the next marker, which points towards a stile in a drystone wall. Go through the stile and take a sharp turn left (south). You now commence

walking along the course of the drystone wall.

(8) The drumlin is below you to the left (east). The drystone wall probably dates from the eighteenth or nineteenth century when the last great drystone wall-building programme took place in Ireland. The wall rises to a height of almost 2m. After about 200m, you come to the end of the wall. Follow the direction of the marker. You will next come to two markers near each other. Both indicate right in the direction of a low cliff face. Make your way across the cliff face.

(9) You may see the raven in flight as you progress. It is the largest member of the crow family and has heavy, black plumage. The raven nests on trees or cliff faces in isolated parts of the country and feeds on carrion. Flocks of golden plovers can also be spotted here, especially in winter when their numbers are boosted by the arrival of winter migrants from Iceland and the Faroe Islands.

Once you have crossed the cliff face, walk along a stone-bordered path. You will reach a drystone wall and you should pass through a stile in the wall as indicated. There is a small group of hawthorn trees growing in a sheltered area just beyond the wall.

Once you have passed through the wall, turn right immediately. Walk parallel to the wall for a couple of hundred metres. You will then pass an ash/hazel copse growing on either side of the wall. You are now walking along the saddle between Slieve Roe to the right and Mullaghmore to the left. Cross over a decayed drystone wall just beyond the woodland and turn left as indicated by a marker. Make the short climb to an erratic with a marker on it indicating left. The next marker is only 15m away and will indicate right. Climb over a ledge and ascend the last 100m to the summit of Mullaghmore (191m).

(10) The large heap of rough stones at the summit is a burial mound. There are approximately twenty such cairns located on the hilltops of the Burren. The Mullaghmore cairn has not been excavated, although

Ballyportry Castle, Corrofin, may be seen from the summit of Mullaghmore.

Mountain avens, a Burren speciality, has a very thin distrubution in Ireland and Britain.
Emma Glanville

excavations of other cairns lead us to believe that there may have been only a small number of persons buried in the Mullaghmore cairn over a long period of time. Excavations elsewhere would suggest the Mullaghmore dead were buried in cists or stone boxes.

Apart from functioning as a funerary space for a select number of people, the Mullaghmore cairn may also have had deep religious significance, given the great effort taken to build it in such a logistically difficult location. The building of the cairn between hilltop and sky may well have meant that it represented a place of communion between this world and the Otherworld.

(11) The grasslands at the summit of Mullaghmore provide sweet, nutritious feed for the cattle in winter. The excellent drainage afforded by the limestone pavement and the rocky pasture is one of the main incentives the farmer has for out-wintering the cattle on the Burren hills. Some of the dead in this hilltop cairn may well have been pioneer farmers in the region up to six millennia ago. In a way this means that there is a remarkably long continuum of pastoral farming on these uplands right through to the present day. In spring the ground here abounds with the delicate lemon-yellow flowers of hoary rockrose. This wildflower is quite rare in Ireland and Great Britain.

(12) Return to the start point by the same outward route via the drumlin and the Famine relief road. When you have reached the relief road again, keep an eye out for small mounds of chipped stones at either side of the trail. During the construction of the road, some of the starving people were engaged to chip stones by hand. When the stones had been chipped to a sufficiently small size, they were placed on the surface of the road. As you near the end of an invigorating hill walk, this may be an ideal moment to pause in silence and imagine the sound of stones being chipped only a few generations ago by starving people in this area of outstanding natural beauty.

Mullaghmore–Slieve Roe–Knockanes

'Mullaghmore mountain is the tabernacle of the Burren …
Once glimpsed it can never be forgotten.'
John O'Donoghue (1993)

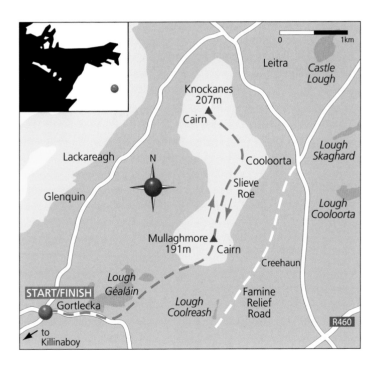

Start/finish: Coming from Corrofin, follow the R476 in the direction of Kilfenora and Lisdoonvarna. Drive 3km from Corrofin until you reach the village of Killinaboy. Take the right turn onto the L1112 opposite Killinaboy's former post office, now known as XPO. Drive 5km down this road until you reach a crossroads. Park at the lay-by on the right just before the crossroads. A display panel at the lay-by contains information regarding the natural heritage of the area.

Description: A very strenuous walk which includes climbing to the summits of three of the Burren's limestone hills, Mullaghmore, Knockanes, Slieve Rua. Much of the walk crosses limestone pavement, which is uneven terrain. The walk is waymarked (blue trail) as far as Mullaghmore summit, the first of the three hills. If you are feeling less energetic, you can just climb Mullaghmore and loop back to the trailhead via the blue trail (7.5 km/3 hours/strenuous).

Highlights: Great views from the summits of parts of north Clare, east Clare and east Galway. Two substantial prehistoric cairns crown the summits of Mullaghmore and Knockanes. Uncommon turlough flora and many different orchid species can be seen during the flowering season.

Distance: 13.5km (8.5 miles)

Time: 5.5 to 6 hours

Grade: Strenuous

Map: *The Burren – a map of the uplands of northwest Clare.* Folding Landscapes. Scale: 1:31,680 or OSI *Discovery Series* Map No.s 51 and 52. Scale: 1:50,000.

Author's note: The walk takes place in the Burren National Park. The park is approximately 1,500 hectares in area and is located in the southeast of the region. It is managed by the NPWS for nature conservation and public access. It is one of six National Parks in the Republic of Ireland.

(1) Walk the 20m from the lay-by to the crossroads. Turn right here along the minor road known as the Crag Road. The first small limestone walking marker on the left indicates a stile entrance to a short, looped nature trail created by the NPWS. This trail does not form part of our Mullaghmore walk.

The Irish government proposed to build a visitor centre in this area in 1991. A group of local and national conservationists opposed the project on the grounds that such a development in an area of outstanding natural beauty would have been inappropriate. Eventually the authorities decided not to grant permission for the project. A car park and a partially built centre were located on the left-hand side of this road and were demolished by court order in 2001.

(2) You come to a green gate on the left, 300m beyond the crossroads. The gate leads into land that is home to a very rich and diverse floral range in spring. The habitat, known as orchid-rich grasslands, has diminished dramatically in the rest of Ireland in the last couple of decades due to intensification of farming.

The land here is grazed in winter by Belted Galloway cattle, so-called because of their wide, white midriff contrasting with their black fore and hindquarters. The 'Belties' are small, hardy cattle with origins in the Scottish lowlands. By grazing these grasslands in winter only, the cattle act as landscape managers, keeping down rough vegetation; they naturally fertilise the landscape and they also leave for summer pastures in time to make way for the flowering season. Farmers are tenants of the NPWS in the National Park and pay a fee for grazing rights.

Belted Galloway: this uncommon beef breed may be seen in the Burren National Park in winter.

You may spot some horses at the opposite side of the road. Oats left out in the field for them attract the attention of the yellowhammer, an uncommon resident bird. The summer male has a bright yellow breast and head. They are found at woodland edges and in areas of overgrown scrub.

(3) The road is bordered on either side by hazel woodland. Walk on for 200m and the woodland gives way to limestone pavement. The open expanse offers one of the most outstanding views in the region. Lough Gealáin (from Irish meaning 'bright lake') is beyond the pavement to your left. The great geological icon of the Burren, the swirling Mullaghmore Hill (191m), provides a dramatic backdrop to the lough. Its layers of rock were laid down below a tropical sea 330 million years ago and were subsequently raised and 'bent' under immense pressure to form the syncline we see today. Knockanes (207m) lies to the north of Mullaghmore.

Lough Gealáin is part lake and part turlough. In dry weather it contracts to a small, water-filled hollow 14m deep. The turlough is filled

Lough Gealáin is part permanent lake and part turlough.
Emma Glanville

from below by springs and empties through swallow holes. Both the springs and swallow holes are situated on the edges of the turlough. The limestone pavement on the edge of the turlough to your left is well worth a visit. The shrubby cinquefoil, whilst nationally rare, abounds here. The five-petal flower is a bright yellow colour. It grows around the winter high-water mark of the turlough. If it looks familiar, this may be because it has been taken to the hearts of the gardening community. The cinquefoil has only one other station in Ireland apart from the Burren and that is on the shores of Lough Corrib in County Galway.

(4) Stroll past the turlough and cross the next stile on your left which has a waymarked post inside it exhibiting red, green and blue discs. You have now walked just over 1km from the crossroads. At the time of writing, there are plans to locate a display board with walking trail information here.

Shrubby cinquefoil grows in only one other region in Ireland apart from the Burren – the shores of Lough Corrib. Emma Glanville

On crossing the stile, you will see a tiny ash tree on your left. Walk along the worn path for 100m until you reach a lone hawthorn on the left of the trail. Cowslips are quite common in this immediate area in spring. This wildflower is becoming increasingly scarce in Ireland and Britain due to the inexorable increase in the use of agri-chemicals. The low-intensity farming regime in the Burren uplands has a crucial role in the continued prosperity of the cowslip here. Other *Primulas* which thrive in the high Burren are the primrose and the false oxlip.

(5) After passing the hawthorn tree, you will soon see the flood debris

which signals the winter high-water mark of the turlough. Keep an eye out for prostrate versions of two of our more uncommon trees as you progress – purging buckthorn and juniper. Both species maintain a low profile on the limestone pavement as part of their adaptation to the depredations of wind in this pitilessly open expanse. Northern bedstraw, marsh dandelion and fen violet are uncommon wildflowers on these islands. However, with careful searching you may be lucky enough to see them here in spring between the summer low-water mark and the winter high-water mark of the Lough Gealáin turlough.

(6) Walk 25m beyond the hawthorn tree in the direction of the turlough edge. Then turn right and start walking northeast in the direction of Mullaghmore Hill.

You are walking along limestone pavement which in this area features the distinctive claw marks of the badger. Phenomenal diggers, badgers come here to sharpen their claws on the pavement. They live in elaborate underground tunnels – setts – which can be up to 200m in length.

Badgers were purposely introduced to Ireland for food and furs approximately 5,000 years ago.

(7) You will pass some slightly raised ground on your left. This area is home to both the bee orchid and the fly orchid in summer. Pollination of the fly orchid is carried out by wasps, which are attracted to the flower by both its appearance and perfume. The perfume cannot be detected by humans. The bee orchid is almost always self-pollinating but can, on rare occasions, be pollinated by bees.

The bee orchid is a self-pollinating flower which has a symbiotic relationship with a fungus called mycorrhiza.

Of particular interest is the Irish orchid – also known as the dense-flowered orchid – *Neotinia maculata*. Its main distribution is Mediterranean. The orchid is called 'Irish' as it is not recorded at all in Britain. In Ireland itself, it is confined to a number of limestone areas in the west. It tends to be the smallest of the orchids, with a delicate whitish-green spike, commonly only 5 cm tall, although taller individuals do occur.

Other orchids to look out for are the early-purple orchid, lesser butterfly orchid, heath spotted-orchid, common spotted-orchid and flecked marsh-orchid. There are twenty-eight orchid species in Ireland, twenty-two of which can be found in the Burren region.

(8) You will next come to a drystone wall just beyond the raised ground. Go through the stile in the wall. The mountain avens can be found in abundance in this area. It is a spectacular wildflower, which usually has eight brilliant white petals surrounding golden stamens. The great natural historian Robert Lloyd Praeger claimed that there were few finer vistas in Ireland than the thousands of hectares of Burren pavement carpeted with mountain avens.

(9) You will pass some hazel scrub on the left of the path. There has been much clearance of hazel by the NPWS staff here in order to protect the rare calcareous grassland and to make it easier for you to walk. You can pick out a yew tree, just above the path on the limestone pavement to your right. The low-sized tree is distinguished by a protective metal cage, one of several cages placed on yew trees in this vicinity by the NPWS to study the impact of browsing by the feral goat population in the Park. One of Ireland's most notable herds of feral goats is located in this region and, with a density of fourteen goats per square kilometre, they are quite a common sight.

There is a fine view of Mullaghmore Hill from here. Mullaghmore and its sister hills, Knockanes and Slieve Roe (188 m), serve as a fine study in glacial erosion, tectonic processes and dissolution by rainwater. The limestone was laid bare by the erosive action of great ice sheets. The terrace and cliff formation was formed by the stripping effect of both water and ice on the weaker points of the rock mass. The huge swirls were created by tectonic movement in the earth's crust, which had the effect of distorting the hills in this southeastern corner of the Burren into a series of folds. The cumulative impact of nature's forces is the formation of one of the most distinctive hills in the country.

(10) Continue along the path and you will shortly turn left as indicated by a marker. As you progress there is now a small turlough below you to your left. The turlough surface is brightened in summer by our largest floating white flower, the white water lily.

There are two unusually shaped rocks at the edge of the turlough, known as mushroom stones, i.e. limestone boulders eroded to a certain height by the dissolving effect of lake water. The rocks clearly show that the turlough spread over a larger area after the last Ice Age when the water table was higher than it is now. Mullaghmore Hill is to your right.

(11) You come to a drystone wall with a gap in it. A lot of hazel has been cut down here by the NPWS in order to make the trail more accessible. Once you pass through the wall, the trail consists of a stone-bordered path. The ground rises slightly. You will see a marker up ahead on a large boulder.

There is hazel scrub off to your right and you can also see the yew-covered bluff at the eastern end of Mullaghmore.

(12) Walk a few hundred metres along the stone-bordered path. You are now walking along one of the terraces of Mullaghmore and up ahead is a large cliff. As you look over to the cliff, you will see a cover of hazel and ash at its base. There is also a fine yew tree growing on the left of the cliff, on its western flank. This specimen is growing to quite a respectable height as it is safe from browsing by the feral goat population.

Continue along the stone-bordered path until you reach the base of the cliff just to the right of the yew. A marker indicates a right turn and the beginning of a steep walk along the base of the cliff face via a cattle-worn path. As you progress in this easterly direction, the trail is bordered on the left-hand side by a hazel/ash/hawthorn copse. At the top of the animal trail turn left as indicated and climb over the small cliff face.

(13) You have climbed onto the second substantial terrace of the hill. A stone-bordered path and animal trail will bring you across the terrace. As you progress you can see another extensive cliff ahead of you. There is a group of hawthorn trees at the base of the cliff to the west, while a drystone wall runs along the eastern face of the cliff. The animal trail will lead you to the base. A marker indicates a right turn at this point and a steep climb via an animal trail. Having climbed 100m along the base of the cliff you will reach the western end of a drystone wall. Continue to ascend for another 100m and then turn left through a gap in the wall as indicated by the marker.

(14) On going through the wall you will see three small cliffs immediately ahead of you. You will also see a large, round cairn just beyond the cliffs at the summit of the hill. Make the short climb to reach the summit.

The cairn consists of a mound of rough stones with a rounded profile. There are approximately twenty such cairns located on the hilltops of the Burren. The Mullaghmore cairn has not been investigated by archaeologists. Poulawack cairn is located near the famous Poulnabrone Dolmen a few kilometres north of here and has been excavated on two occasions. The Poulawack excavations revealed the remains of only eighteen people. The majority of the remains are contained in cists. Poulawack functioned as a burial mound during the Stone Age and Bronze Age, so we may conclude that the cairns served in part as sacred places for the special dead.

(15) The grasslands at the summit of Mullaghmore provide sweet, nutritious feed for the cattle in winter. The excellent drainage afforded by the limestone pavement and the rocky pasture is one of the main incentives the farmer has for out-wintering the cattle on the Burren hills. The ground here also abounds in spring with the delicate lemon-yellow flowers of hoary rockrose.

Two of our most common falcons, the kestrel and the peregrine falcon, can be seen on occasion on this hilltop. The kestrel hunts by hovering motionless in mid-air whereas the peregrine circles at great heights and then dives at amazing speed with its wings held tightly to its body. The peregrine is the fastest hunter in Ireland, reaching speeds of over 200km/h. (16) Mullaghmore offers excellent views of the hinterland. The dwelling used as the parochial house in the ecclesiastical TV comedy series *Father Ted* is due west of the peak. To the northeast, you can see the 400-million-year-old Sandstones of Slieve Aughty in east Galway which are crowned by a huge wind farm; to the east is Mahera, a hill in east Clare topped by a television transmitter; also to the east but in the foreground is Lough Bunny, the largest lake in the east Burren wetlands. The lake is 195 hectares in area and much of it is surrounded by limestone pavement.

(17) On leaving the cairn, head northeast towards the summit of Slieve Roe. You are now actually walking along a cleft in the grasslands. When you have walked 200m from the cairn you will see a marker below you to your left.

Descend towards the marker by an animal trail. A drystone wall comes into view in the col between the two peaks below you. You come to a ledge and walk down the short distance from the ledge to the marker. Turn left at the marker and walk 20m to the next marker, which is placed on an erratic. Head straight downhill from the erratic to the drystone wall in the col. Climb over a low section of the wall by the ash copse on your right.

(18) As you face Slieve Roe, walk a few hundred metres to your left in a westerly direction across the terrace from the ash copse. You are walking just above Slieve Roe's lowest cliff. Continue to the western end of the terrace in order to reach a point in the next cliff that is easy to climb. You subsequently negotiate two more cliffs before reaching the summit. Walk over both these cliffs along their lower western flanks. Skaghard Castle was one of the medieval strongholds of the O'Brien clan and you can see it to the northeast of the Slieve Roe peak. The lake to the left of the castle is Castle Lough.

(19) Knockanes is to the northwest and can soon be reached by crossing the saddle between it and Slieve Roe. Knockanes also has a cairn on its summit. A lot of effort must have gone into constructing these hilltop cairns, given their sheer scale and the remoteness of their location. Turloughmore Mountain to the north also contains several cairns on the hilltops along its range.

(20) Return to the walk start/finish point from Knockanes by the same route across the hills of Slieve Roe and Mullaghmore.

Burren Way

'I named you for all the wildflowers of the Burren I had seen in one day.'
Michael Longley, 'The Ice Cream Man' (2006)

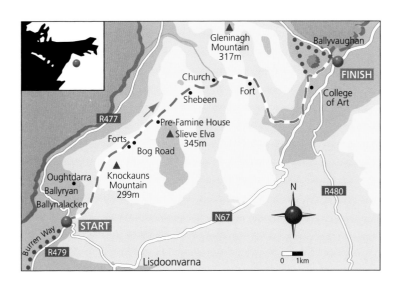

Start and finish: The start point of the walk is in Ballynalackan at the junction of the R477 going northwest from Lisdoonvarna and the R479 going north from Doolin. The walk starts on the minor road to the left of the entrance gates of Ballynalackan Castle Hotel (as you face the hotel). It ends in the village of Ballyvaughan. As the walk is linear, it would be ideal to leave a car in Ballyvaughan and get a lift or taxi to the start point. There is also a Bus Éireann daily service between Ballyvaughan and Doolin, which is 5km southwest of the start point.

Description: The Burren Way is a 123km linear walking route which eventually links with the Mid-Clare Way south of Corrofin village. The waymarked trail consists of old cattle tracks and minor roads. Level gradient mostly but the walk does include one steep gradient.

Highlights: Stunning views of the Clare and Galway coastlines. Medieval castles and churches, ring forts. Rich and varied range of Burren wildflowers. Limestone and shale uplands, fertile valleys.

Distance: 22km (13.5 miles)

Time: 6.5 hours

Grade: Strenuous

Map: *The Burren – a map of the uplands of northwest Clare.* Folding Landscapes. Scale: 1:31,680 or OSI *Discovery Series* Map No. 51. Scale: 1:50,000.

(1) There is a Burren Way information panel at the start of the trail. The first 3km of the trail are along a minor surfaced road. Ballynalackan Castle Hotel, a nineteenth-century house, and its grounds are beyond the trees on the right as you begin. The ruins of the medieval castle of Ballynalackan are beside the hotel. When building this stronghold, the powerful O'Brien family made excellent use of the natural attributes of the land, building the castle on the precipice of a cliff, thus making it very difficult to attack. It is also at a historically important access point to the region. More than half of the twenty-one medieval castles in the Burren were built on the frontier between the Burren and the outside world, which suggests that they were strategically located at access points in order to defend the occupants' precious winter pastures in the well-drained Burren uplands.

(2) At the 1.5km mark, the road dips appreciably. Emerging from the dip,

A green road in the north of the Burren. Green roads were built to facilitate the droving of livestock.

you will have great views of the hinterland. The Cliffs of Moher are to the southwest and the Aran Islands are due west. As you progress, the scrub-covered valley of Oughtdarra is on your left (west) below you. Oughtdarra was farmed for several millennia, until it was abandoned a couple of decades ago; hazel scrub has now established itself in the absence of grazing. The Oughtdarra scrub is a haven for songbirds and is also home to Ireland's arboreal 'cat', the pine marten. There is much evidence of Early Christian settlement in the valley including ring forts and the ruins of St Mac Dara's church.

The extensive limestone pavement area between Oughtdarra and the sea is known as Ballyryan. The maritime flora here, added to its rich and varied Arctic/Alpine/Mediterranean range, make the area one of the most botanically significant in the Burren. The pyramidal bugle is a Burren speciality and its only Burren station is on the rocks at Ballyryan. This Alpine flower is rare in Ireland and Britain.

(3) The surfaced road gives way to a green road, which was originally built as a droving road for cattle. It is still used by farmers to gain access to their cattle and sheep and is also used as a walking route.

You now walk along an extensive plateau for several kilometres overlooking Galway Bay. Knockauns Mountain (299m) is to your right and is part of the shale outcrop, including Slieve Elva and Poulacapple, which runs northeast from here. Shale is composed of either mud or clay and was deposited on top of the limestone from ancient seas about 300 million years ago. The limestone pavements of the Burren uplands were stripped of their shale cover during the last Ice Age. However, Knockauns, Slieve Elva and Poulacapple were unaffected by glacial stripping as they projected above the great ice sheets. Such isolated rocks are known as nunataks, from the Eskimo word *nunataq*.

The slopes of Knockauns are heavily planted with conifers, which are not native to Ireland. These conifers are quite a common sight on wet, acidic lands throughout the country – a consequence of the state's forestry subsidisation policy. The conifers are native to Scandinavia and North America. They mature quickly here thanks to the climatic and soil conditions. However, whilst they may make short-term economic sense, the plantations are of far less biodiversity value than our own native hardwoods.

(4) The green road stretches for 2km and it then merges with a surfaced road. Walk along this road for half a kilometre. You arrive at a junction where the surfaced road veers left (west) down to the sea. However, you continue straight on along the trail as indicated by the marker. You are now on another section of the green road. There are two ring forts in the field to your right: Cathair Bheag ('the small fort') and Cathair Mhaol ('the bare fort').

Ring forts are made of stone or earth. The term 'fort' is grandiose as the structures were in essence fortified farmsteads, which would not have survived sustained attack. The ring fort is Ireland's most common field monument, with up to 40,000 of them in the country. Most date from AD 500 to AD 1000.

There are approximately 450 ring forts in the Burren alone – a testament to the area's agricultural importance. It is still not altogether clear why such a huge number of individual dispersed farm strongholds were built in such a relatively short space of time.

The Alpine spring gentian with its brilliant blue flowers is an icon of the Burren.

(5) Walk along the green road for 1km. You will pass some fuchsia hedging on the trail before a cottage where the green road merges onto a surfaced road at the cottage. Walk along the surfaced road for 150m until you reach a junction. Our trail goes back onto another stretch of the green road here as indicated by a marker. The surfaced road, however, descends left (west) to the coast. The Burren Way is noted for its fine coastal vistas and, if you look west, you will see Galway Bay, the Aran Islands and Connemara.

(6) You pass through a gate and stile just 40m into this section of the green road. This is the first of six gates and stiles you will pass through before you descend into

the Caher Valley. The ruin of a stone house, which fell into disuse only the in 1960s, is on the right of the trail half a kilometre beyond the gate. A further half a kilometre on, you pass through a second gate and stile. The high ground on the right has a very wide floral range in spring, including the spring gentian and the early-purple orchid. A tincture from the root of the gentian was used by herbalists in the past to relieve sore throats. The gentian root is also the main ingredient in the potent Italian grappa called genzianella. I can confirm it is a bitter affair!

Orchids have been associated with fertility and love from Classical times. The word 'orchid' derives from the Greek word for testicle. Indeed, the Irish word for the orchid, *magairlín*, means the same thing. In Brian Merriman's epic 18th-century poem, '*Cúirt An Mheán Oíche*' (The Midnight Court), the early-purple orchid is resorted to by Irish women as a love charm, exasperated as they are by the lack of romance in Irish men.

(7) You soon pass a second house in ruins on the right, mapped as a pre-Famine dwelling. The structure is historically significant as most of the pre-Famine dwellings in the Burren were made of perishable materials and no longer survive. According to the 1841 census over 85 per cent of all dwellings in the Burren were fourth classification ('all mud cabins having only one room').

The ruins of Faunarooska Castle are below to the left (west) of the trail. The castle was one of the strongholds of the O'Lochlann family. They were Gaelic landowning aristocrats who governed the north of the Burren in medieval times. On your right is Slieve Elva (345m), an extensive shale outcrop like Knockauns. The trail follows the geological interface between the shale and limestone. The rush-covered fields signify shale bedrock. Rush is the icon of waterlogged soil and is absent from the well-drained limestone land.

(8) There is a track deviating right (east) towards Slieve Elva. However, continue straight along the green road. The third gate and stile are 400m beyond this junction. There are more non-native conifer plantations on

the slopes of Slieve Elva to the right. The fourth gate and stile are a further 300m along the trail. A lone hawthorn is in the field to the left as you approach the gate. Its shape has been heavily distorted by the ravages of the Atlantic winds. Birds feed on the berries or 'haws' of the tree and insects visit both the

A drystone wall with stile along the Burren Way. berries and flowers.

(9) The fifth gate and stile are half a kilometre further along the trail. It is well worth pausing here to look at the limestone pavement on the left of the trail. The pavements are known as 'clints' and the fractures as 'grikes'. The fractures are being continually widened, dissolved by rainwater, which naturally picks up a carbonic acid on passing through the atmosphere. Many wildflowers more commonly associated with woodland (including tutsan and honeysuckle) grow in the grikes as they find humid and shady conditions there. The grikes also provide shelter from the wind and protection from grazing animals.

The Burren is home to two different species of heather – bell heather and ling or common heather. It is a wonderful spectacle in late summer to see the purple-red flowers of bell heather and the pink flowers of ling set against the backdrop of the limestone pavement. Heather cannot tolerate calcium and so the heathers in the Burren actually grow in peaty hummocks devoid of calcium – tiny ghettoes of acid soil in the great alkaline expanse of limestone. Renowned Irish botanist David Webb said that one of the enduring fascinations of Burren flora was the phenomenon of lime-hating and lime-loving plants growing in proximity to each other.

(10) You soon pass through the sixth and final gate and stile on the trail. Look back west from this vantage point to be rewarded with a breathtaking vista of Galway Bay, Connemara, the Aran Islands and the Atlantic Ocean.

The Burren's limestone uplands are used as rocky pasture from November to May each year. The excellent drainage afforded by the pavement and the thin soils mean that many local farmers opt to transfer the cattle to the hills in winter rather than house them in the valleys. Although this is the more labour-intensive option, the cattle are healthier and more valuable as a result. There is also the huge ecological dividend of the emergence of beautiful wildflowers on the hills in spring, thanks to the cattle suppressing vigorous grasses and scrub in winter. This form of transhumance is the opposite of that which takes place in the Alps and Pyrenees, where cattle are transferred to the heights in summer.

(11) You pass another ruin on your right, an abandoned 'shebeen' (illicit drinking house). The word shebeen comes from the Irish *séibe*, meaning mug. You then reach the end of the plateau. Before beginning the descent into the Caher Valley, take a moment to soak in the great views of Galway Bay and Connemara to the west, the Burren hills to the north and the valley itself below you.

It is worth noting the important role which farming plays in shaping the landscape. In contrast to the winter grazing that takes place on the uplands, much of the farming in the Caher Valley is intensive. The large fields with improved grasslands are dedicated to summer pasture and silage production.

There is an extensive area of hazel scrub to the east of the valley where farming has been abandoned altogether and the area is returning to its natural state, i.e. woodland.

(12) Start your descent into the valley. You soon come to a very sharp elbow and the trail veers right. A juniper tree on the left of the trail is sheltered from the wind by a drystone wall. The word 'gin' comes from the Dutch word for juniper – *genever* – and gin is, in fact, made by flavouring a white spirit with juniper berries. Hawthorn, bramble and bracken encroach upon the trail as you near the floor of the valley.

(13) The ruins of Formoyle church (including Gothic windows) are on the left just before the green road merges with a surfaced road. Cross the Caher River bridge. Walk 150m to a T-junction. Turn right here as indicated by the marker and almost immediately turn left back onto the green road, again as indicated by a marker.

You are now climbing a steep pass between two hills. The ascent will bring you to the great ruin of Caheranardurrish Fort, situated at the top of the pass. The fort is strategically located on well-drained land with commanding views of the surrounding countryside. There are the ruins of a mass house and a shebeen within the fort, which must have once catered for the spiritual and venal needs of the local populace. The fort is bivallate (i.e. the living quarters were enclosed within two concentric walls). Whilst some forts are even trivallate, the majority of them are univallate. The elite in society commissioned their underlings to construct the forts in part as tribute to them. It may have been felt that the more elaborate the structure, the greater the tribute.

(14) You soon begin the 1km descent to a junction, where you turn right, as indicated. Now begin walking through the fertile Feenagh Valley on another minor surfaced road. Look up to your left (north) to see a ring fort on either side of a track. The fort on the right is known as Lios Mac Síoda ('Sheedy's fort'). It was built on the precipice of a cliff to make the occupants and their cattle even more secure from attack by rival clans or wolves.

(15) A couple of kilometres beyond the junction is Gragan's Wood. It is deciduous woodland, which is the natural woodland of Ireland, and as such has enormous value in terms of flora and fauna. Ireland's land area has no more than 1.5 per cent deciduous woodland cover.

Keep an eye out in the hedgerows along the road for native shrubs and trees such as spindle, blackthorn and whitethorn. Spindle is a shrub or small tree with a hard timber that was used in the past to make spindles. In autumn its pink fruits split to reveal orange seeds. You will pass an unsurfaced road on the right with a chestnut tree on either side. This road leads to the bog on the shale-covered Poulacapple Hill and is the subject of Route 8 (Bog Road).

(16) The Rathborney River runs parallel to the road for a short distance as the trail goes through the fertile Rathborney Valley. The roofless Catholic

A ruined cottage on the Burren Way between Ballynalackan and Ballyvaughan.

church of Rathborney is on the right as you progress, with a laneway leading to it. The church dates from the sixteenth century and the high quality of its stonework is evident in the intricate detail surrounding the windows. Many local people who died from famine-related illnesses are buried in these grounds. The nearby Ballyvaughan Valley had a population of over 150 people per square kilometre prior to the Famine in the 1840s.

You soon pass Glenraha Chapel on your right. An inscription on the west gable reads, 'This chapel was built at the sole expense of the most Noble Marquis of Buckingham in 1795 for the advantage of his tenants.' The chapel served as the local Catholic church until the 1860s when the current church was built in Ballyvaughan. You have now passed four chapels in the last 5km of the trail – Formoyle, Caheranardurrish Mass house, Rathborney and Glenraha – so it will come as no surprise to learn that the Burren region, which is 350 square kilometres in area, has the highest concentration of ecclesiastical sites in Ireland.

(17) You come to a junction about half a kilometre beyond Glenraha. Turn left as indicated by the marker and continue along another minor road. There are many holly trees growing on limestone pavement at either side. Holly is a tough tree and can tolerate the exposed ground of the Burren. The young shoots of holly were once used as fodder for livestock.

(18) The cylindrical Newtown Castle on the right is part of the complex of buildings that make up the Burren College of Art. The occupants of Newtown in medieval times were members of the extended O'Lochlann family, whose kingdom was situated here in the north of the Burren and this particular stronghold is located in the fertile Ballyvaughan Valley.

Newtown, which is in very good condition, is known as a castle or tower house even though it was essentially a fortified farmhouse. There are approximately 3,000 such castles in Ireland and only 30 of them are cylindrical in shape. However, Newtown is unique as it is the only cylindrical tower house in Ireland to sit on a square base.

There is hazel woodland on either side of the road beyond the college which gives way to grasslands and the view opens out to Ballyvaughan Valley and Ailwee Hill (251 m) to the right (east). Moneen (263 m) is the hill to the north of Ailwee.

(19) You come to a junction 800m beyond the college. Turn right here as indicated by the marker. Walk a short distance until you reach a marker which indicates left. Go through the stile in the drystone wall here. Walk across the field until you reach some hazel woodland. You now walk through a mosaic of woodland and limestone pavement until you reach good pastureland. This area is transformed from pasture to turlough (temporary water body) from time to time. In periods of high rainfall and high tides, the spring water cannot go underground because of the build-up of seawater below. Thus, the water lodges on the surface and the turlough is formed. Turloughs are almost unique in the world to certain limestone areas in the west and centre of Ireland. This section of the trail may be impassable occasionally.

By the community sports field, you reach a gravel path that leads onto a surfaced road. Pass the local national school on the right. The end of this road forms a junction with the coast road. Turn right here and walk the couple of hundred metres to the end of the trail in the picturesque village of Ballyvaughan.

Caher Valley Loop

'She arrived …teaching us the fish in the rock, the fern's bewildered tenderness deep in the fissure.'

Séamus Heaney, 'An Aisling in the Burren' (1984)

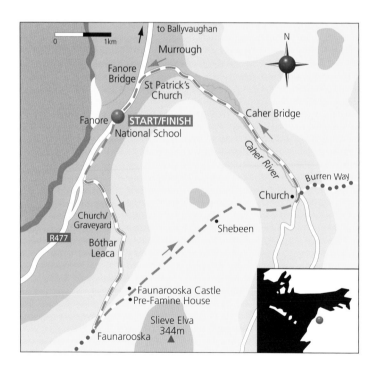

Start/finish: Fanore Beach car park, 2km north of Fanore village on the left-hand side of the R477 between Fanore and Ballyvaughan.

Description: A long but moderate waymarked loop along a river valley and an old cattle track known as a green road (an unsurfaced road). The walk is mostly along minor roads and the **green road.**

Highlights: Outstanding views of the north of the Burren, Galway Bay, the Aran Islands and Connemara. The Arctic/Alpine/ Mediterranean range of Burren flora. Church and castle ruins. Hundreds of hectares of limestone pavement.

Distance: 14.5km (9 miles)

Time: 4 hours

Grade: Moderate

Map: *The Burren – a map of the uplands of northwest Clare.* Folding Landscapes. Scale: 1:31,680 or OSI *Discovery Series* Map No. 51. Scale: 1:50,000.

(1) Most of County Clare's coastline is rocky so Fanore Beach is a crowded, happy resort in good summer weather. The beach has an idyllic location looking out at the Aran Islands and south Connemara. On leaving the car park, turn right. Take the next turn left at the Fanore National School (1968). The original National School building (1887) in the parish is now a

Fanore Beach and caravan park from the air. Emma Glanville

private residence. Take the next turn left onto the minor road known as Bóthar Leaca, which translates as the Flaggy Road. You now start your 4km modest ascent to the Fanore green road.

(2) At the 3km mark along Bóthar Leaca, the ruins of Faunarooska tower house/castle are in a field to the left. The castle was just one of many in the kingdom of the O'Lochlanns in north Clare in medieval times. The structure is unusual in that it is cylindrical in shape. The vast majority of the approximately 3,000 tower houses in Ireland are rectangular. Looking seawards below you are splendid ruins of the eleventh-century Killonaghan church. There would have been much traffic between the castle and the church in medieval times as the political and religious élite enjoyed a good relationship. There are at least six ring forts in a very compact area a kilometre north of the castle. The Burren is estimated to house about 450 ring forts – a reflection of the wealth and power of the region in Early Christian times.

The east-facing altar window of the medieval ruins of Killonaghan church in Fanore.

(3) Ascend for another kilometre, then turn left on to the green road. The road is an ancient cattle highway of indeterminate age. It now forms part of the Burren Way, a 123km linear walking route which eventually links up with the Mid-Clare Way south of Corrofin village. A 22km section of the Way is the subject of Route 5 (p. 35).

(4) You soon come to a gate and stile. Cross over the stile. Immediately, there is a steep bank on the right. It is quite exciting to pause here in springtime to see warm-climate plants like the early-purple orchid mingling with the Alpine spring gentian. The mix of wildflowers from different climatic zones and habitats in the world fascinates plant fans and experts alike. Renowned botanist and author Bob Gibbons' book *Wildflower Wonders*

Yarrow being pollinated by a fly.

46

of the World (2011) profiles fifty outstanding botanical sites on earth and includes the Burren.

Heather, yarrow, self-heal, harebell, devil's-bit scabious and tormentil are all common along this section of the Burren Way in the flowering season.

(5) The trail continues in the shadow of the shale-capped Slieve Elva (344m) off to the right. Shale is composed of either mud or clay and was deposited on top of the limestone from ancient seas about 300 million years ago. The limestone pavements of the Burren uplands were stripped of their shale cover during the last Ice Age. However, Slieve Elva remained unaffected by the glacial stripping as it projected above the great ice sheets. Such isolated rocks are known as nunataks, from the Eskimo word *nunataq*.

(6) There are two stone houses in ruins on the right of the trail. Both were abandoned as recently as the 1960s. The second house is mapped as a pre-Famine dwelling and is historically significant as most of the pre-Famine dwellings in the Burren were made of perishable materials and no longer survive. According to the 1841 census over 85 per cent of all dwellings in the Burren were fourth classification ('all mud cabins having only one room').

(7) At the 1.5km mark along this section of the Burren Way is a junction with a track leading off to the right. However, you continue straight on. As you approach the next gate and stile, there are a large number of tall limestone slabs embedded in the clints (fissures) of the limestone pavement. Although groups of these 'verticals' are common in the Burren uplands, academic discussion on them has been limited. They most probably served as waymarkers in the past on either secular or pilgrimage routes. Many routeways tended to be cross-country and much rougher than they are today. The 'verticals' would have been important navigation landmarks in times of bad weather and poor visibility. They are not to be confused with their modern equivalent erected by narcissistic visitors in some of the Burren's tourist 'honeypot' sites.

(8) You will pass a modest stone structure in ruins on the right-hand side of the trail. It is an abandoned shebeen, an illicit drinking house. The word 'shebeen' comes from the Irish *séibe* which means mug. The long, flat stretch of walking soon ends and the descent to the floor of Caher River valley beckons. However, before you descend take a few moments to soak in the wonderful views as you face the valley. Galway Bay is to the west; the great limestone hills of Gleninagh and Cappanwalla are due north and northeast respectively; the Slieve Aughty sandstone hill range is off in the distance to the east. Caher Valley is now sparsely populated. However, there were up to 200 people per square mile living in the valley prior to the Great Famine of 1845–1849. The severe depopulation caused by the Famine would suggest

that the vast majority of the people lived in one-roomed mud cabins on a diet of potatoes and milk. Death or emigration was their fate.

(9) Note another group of 'verticals' on your left as you descend. When you arrive on the valley floor, the ruin of the parish church of Formoyle is to the left of the track. The church fell into disuse not long after the Famine. Note the walled-in Gothic windows in the south of the building. There is a holy well, Tobar Bhrain, a couple of hundred metres north of the church. The track gives way to a minor road. Cross the Caher River bridge. The river is the only consistent overground river system in the region as its riverbed consists of a layer of impermeable boulder clay. All other Burren rivers are either subterranean or intermittently overground due to the permeable nature of the limestone. The Caher River empties into the sea at Fanore beach. You soon approach a T-junction. *At this point, you may turn right if you wish to follow the Black Head Loop (see Route 7, p. 50), which is a longer and more strenuous walk.* To continue on the Caher Valley Loop, Turn left here onto a minor road.

(10) You are now walking west through the valley, heading towards the sea. Continue for 2km and cross the river again. The house on the left has a remarkable riverside garden which is open to visitors by appointment. Look below the bridge where there is a large number of white stones in the riverbed. The stones have a white crust of calcium carbonate. The river offers good breeding habitats for the dipper and the grey wagtail. The wagtail is distinguished by its yellow flanks whilst both birds like nesting under bridges.

(11) Just over a kilometre further on the road merges with the riverbank. There are some spectacular deposits along the bank – boulders, stones and clay. The clay has a flora rich in black bog rush and juniper. This landform is the result of glacial deposition. Much of this western part of the valley is subject to soil creep (the slow downslope movement of soil under the influence of gravity) which lessens its agricultural value. The valley is known locally as the Khyber Pass. The extravagant moniker for

Surfers on Fanore beach. Eoin Walsh

this small gorge between two hills was given by an RIC officer who had seen service in the great pass along the Afghanistan–Pakistan border.

(12) St Patrick's church (built in 1870) is on the left as you progress. You will also pass a period two-storey house on your left, which was formerly the Royal Irish Constabulary (RIC) barracks. RIC barracks in rural Ireland were often rented houses like this one. The constabulary was the direct instrument of British rule in Ireland for much of the nineteenth and early twentieth centuries. It was responsible for the enforcement of land evictions in the nineteenth century and was very unpopular amongst the rural poor.

(13) You arrive at the junction with the R477 coastal road. Turn left and walk for less than a kilometre in single file facing oncoming traffic. The Fanore beach car park will be on your right.

ROUTE 7:

Black Head Loop

'There is the sea up in parabolas of foam, above the rocks, the town in nestling limestone under wing.'
Michael Hartnett, 'Secular Prayers' (1967).

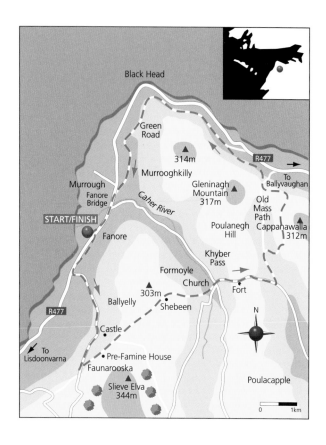

Start/finish: Fanore beach car park, 2km north of Fanore village on the left-hand side of the R477 between Fanore and Ballyvaughan.

Description: A waymarked, looped walk featuring a minor road, green roads, tracks and mountain paths.

Highlights: Outstanding views of the north of the Burren, Galway Bay, the Aran Islands and Connemara. The Arctic/Alpine/ Mediterranean range of Burren flora. Church and castle ruins. Hundreds of hectares of limestone pavement

Distance: 26km (16 miles)

Time: 6.5 hours

Grade: Strenuous

Map: *The Burren – a map of the uplands of northwest Clare.* Folding Landscapes. 1:31,680 or OSI *Discovery Series* Map No. 51. Scale: 1:50,000.

For points (1) to (10) of this walk, see Route 6, on p. 44, Caher Valley Loop.

When you arrive at the T-junction mentioned in (10) of Route 6, turn right and almost immediately turn left. You are now back on an unsurfaced track. A modest ascent takes you from the lush Caher Valley back to the stony uplands.

(11) When your climb is completed, you will see a substantial ring fort on your right in a field. Cathair an Ard Dorais ('the fort of the high door') is actually bivallate, i.e. it has not one but two ringed enclosures. Remains of the outer enclosure are still visible. A greater number of enclosures would have been built by the lower economic orders as a form of greater tribute to the elite. The forts tend to be built on elevated ground for security reasons and good land is rarely far away. Cathair an Ard Dorais must be the only ring fort in Ireland which houses a chapel and shebeen! These modest temples of God and Bacchus are probably nineteenth century in origin.

(12) Begin your descent into the next valley of Rathborney. The fertile valleys of the Burren are nearly all dedicated to grasslands. The prime agricultural activity is beef farming, centred on the production of young live animals for export. Burren beef is a premium product. As you descend along the track you can pick out the stone forts of Cathair Fhiodhnaith and Lios Mac Síoda on the slopes of Cappanawalla at the other side of the valley. Both forts are strategically situated at the interface between

51

the valley (summer grazing) and the rocky uplands (winter grazing). Both monuments are also under threat from the advance of scrub due to the decline of winter grazing in the hills in the last couple of decades.

(13) Once in the valley, turn left along a minor road and go through a gate and stile. Pass a house on your left and you will soon veer right on to a track which takes you west along the slopes of Cappanawalla Hill. You may be able to spot faint traces of an old Mass track going through the field sytems below on the valley floor. The track was used formerly by people from Rathborney Valley and beyond going to the parish church of Gleninagh Valley, west of here. These Cappanawalla slopes are carpeted with wildflowers in spring, making it one of the most stunning botanical sites in the region. The Arctic/Apline/Mediterranean mosaic is all on display here with a profusion of mountain

avens, spring gentians and early-purple orchids.

(14) Having walked along the slopes for 2.5km, pass through a gate to meet with outstanding views. Looking seaward, Galway Bay and Connemara are to the north. Galway city is visible to the northeast whilst Ballyvaughan Bay is to the east. The valley below is Gleninagh. The

Time out overlooking Gleninagh Valley and Galway Bay.

medieval O'Lochlann castle had a strategic location on the shore as some of the principal 'highways' in medieval times were on water.

There was a lot of trade between Connemara and Gleninagh (one of the last Irish-speaking areas in County Clare) in the past. Turf was the main product landing at Gleninagh pier from Connemara. The trail veers left and you eventually pass through a drystone wall on your right. You then descend along a track (part of the Mass path) till directed left by the waymark.

(15) You now proceed westwards for a distance of over 2km. Herculean work has been done here by local landowners in cutting away the scrub and making the trail passable. The long, linear wall by your side as you progress serves as a townland boundary, the townland being the smallest geographical unit in Ireland. The Burren is home to several thousand kilometres of drystone walls. Most of those in pristine condition probably date from 1760 to 1850 when a raft of Land Enclosure Acts in the UK and Ireland succeeded in legislatively denying ordinary people access to private land.

(16) You eventually turn right and descend a short distance to a green road. Turning left here, your direction is still west as you walk along the slopes of the Dobhach Bhrainín hill (314m) which is known locally as Murrough

(it is Murrooghkilly on the map). The Burren is home to an astonishing thirty of Ireland's thirty-two butterfly species (the Burren region accounts for only 1 per cent of Ireland's land mass). Species recorded along this green road include the small blue, small copper, the common blue, small heath, dark green fritillary, speckled wood, meadow brown, grayling, small tortoiseshell, peacock and the whites (green-veined, large, small and wood).

(17) The trail veers around Black Head, the region's most famous promontory. You are now on the homeward stretch, walking southwards and enjoying the sublime coastal views along Galway Bay. The green road is also renowned for the richness and diversity of its wildflower species. There is an abundance of orchids along the trail, including bee orchid, pyramidal orchid, fragrant orchid and autumn lady's tresses. Very uncommon species in Ireland and the UK such as hoary rock rose, maidenhair fern and Arctic sandwort all thrive in the vicinity as well. Arctic sandwort was first discovered in the Burren in 1961 and was not identified again until 2008.

The white flower is so tiny that the chances of finding it are remote. The plant is known at only a couple of other stations in these islands. Other plants to look out for are burnet rose, bloody crane's-bill, spring gentian, mountain avens and lime-hating heathers.

Winter-pasture cattle on Black Head.

(18) As you near the end of the green road you will see a monstrous erratic on the right of the trail with another boulder lying beside it. The smaller boulder is home to the fossilised remains of marine invertebrates called brachiopods. These creatures inhabited a warm tropical sea hundreds of millions of years ago. On decaying and falling to the sea floor the brachiopods' skeletons embedded in calcium carbonate. Compacting subsequently occurred and thus the limestone rock was formed.

(19) The green road ends at a drystone wall with stile. You now descend 0.5km along a minor road. On arriving at a T-junction, turn left and walk the last kilometre along the coast road R477 back to the trailhead at Fanore beach car park. Face oncoming traffic and walk in single file. If you conclude your walk in fine summer weather, you might reward yourself with a dip in the sea.

Bog Road

*'Bog cotton threading the verges
May tempt me from the path to browse.'*
Gerard Fanning, *Canower Sound* (2003)

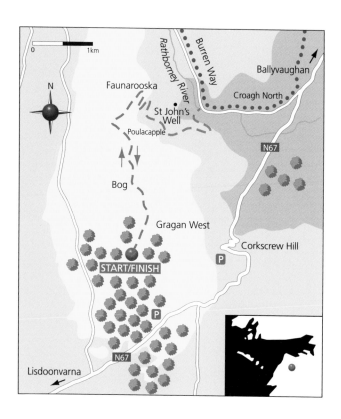

Start/finish: Follow the N67 from Ballyvaughan going towards Lisdoonvarna. Drive over the winding, hilly roadway known as Corkscrew Hill, approximately 5.5km from Ballyvaughan. Take the second turn right after the Corkscrew onto a forest road, signed Burren Way. Pass the telecommunications antennae on the left. There is ample parking at the next junction. Continue on foot to the second junction and turn right (north) up this track indicated by a footpath sign. This is the starting point of the Bog Road.

Description: A linear, downhill walk along an unsurfaced road from the Poulacapple hilltop to the valley of Rathborney including the return (uphill) from valley to hilltop to the start point. (You may, of course, exercise the option of being collected by car in the Rathborney Valley, thus obviating the need to do the walk in reverse.)

Highlights: Magnificent views of the north Burren hills and valleys as well as strong contrasts in scenery and vegetation afforded by the shale and limestone uplands.

Distance: 10km (6.2 miles)

Time: 3.5 hours

Grade: Moderate

Map: *The Burren – a map of the uplands of northwest Clare.* Folding Landscapes. Scale: 1:31,680 or OSI *Discovery Series* Map No. 51. Scale: 1:50,000.

(1) You have commenced the walk along the shale uplands of Poulacapple Mountain. Poulacapple is one of three mountains in the Burren (the other two are Knockauns and Slieve Elva) to have retained its shale-capping above the limestone. Whilst limestone was formed 335 to 360 million years ago, shale subsequently formed on top of the limestone 320 to 330 million years ago. These shale hills protruded above the glaciers and escaped the stripping action of the great ice sheets during the last Ice Age.

(2) The wet, spongy and poorly drained ground you see along the trail is blanket bog and it makes for one of the most remarkable characteristics of Irish scenery. It is quite a rare eco-system worldwide but not in Ireland, and is host to common and also to some rare flora and fauna. Blanket bogs formed in upland areas of the west of Ireland about 4,000 years ago. The climate became much wetter and heavy rainfall leached minerals from the soil which, in turn, formed an impermeable iron pan. The soil above

A turf tile – a drystone construction for the drying of fuel such as turf.

the iron pan was waterlogged and peat was formed in the wet, oxygen-deficient conditions. Peat is 90 per cent water but also includes the partially decomposed remains of dead plant material, including mosses, grasses and heathers. Bog myrtle, heather and purple moor grass can be seen flourishing here in spring.

(3) At the half-kilometre mark, you may see turf (extracted peat) stacked in small clumps at the side of the trail for drying in late summer. Most peat is now extracted by machine although it is still harvested by hand to a limited extent using an implement called a *sleán* (a traditional turf spade or slane). Turf is used in domestic fires – it is a fossil fuel just like coal and gas.

(4) After 750m, you reach a four-lane junction. The road to the right has recently been surfaced in stone. The lane to the left is one of many bog *bóithríní* or lanes along the trail. Lanes like this enabled local people with turbary rights to access the peatlands in order to harvest turf. Turbary (from Old French *tourbe*, meaning 'turf') rights entitle the individual to cut turf for fuel. The Poulacapple peatlands were very rich in lore and life up to the 1960s when many people from the fuel-starved valleys of Rathborney and Ballyvaughan exercised their turbary rights to the full. Very little turf is now harvested in Poulacapple. The advent of oil-fired central heating and changed lifestyles may explain in part the demise of the tradition. Go straight on through this four-lane junction.

(5) As you progress, note the large cutaway bank created by mechanised peat harvesting on the right of the trail. The soil nearest the top of the bank is better drained and heather grows in this area. Nearby, deer grass and

purple moor grass grow on the more poorly drained land. Wild angelica, devil's-bit scabious, meadowsweet and knapweed are much in evidence on the margins of the trail itself where there are more nutrients. The Burren hill to the right of the trail, off to the east, is Ailwee (251 m).

(6) It is a 0.75km stroll to the next junction. Another narrow bog lane veers off to the left here. Turn right and follow the trail. The long, white, silky hairs of the cotton grasses are a glorious sight from May to July each year. Common cotton grass, aka bog cotton, is our most abundant cotton grass with several plumes of feathery seeds, whereas hare's-tail cotton grass is the only cotton grass with a single, erect head. The yellow flower of bog asphodel is another visual delight.

(7) Stroll on for another half a kilometre and you will reach a metal gate. Hawthorn trees do not grow on acidic soil so the wind-bent hawthorns beyond the gate dramatically foretell the imminent change in the landscape from shale to limestone, and from acid to alkaline soil.

(8) There are a couple of huge fence posts to the left of the trail, 20m after the gate. The green, tangled mass hanging from the fence posts is the lichen *Usnea*. Its presence is testament to the purity of the air in these uplands. It is more commonly seen hanging down from dead trunks and branches in woodland. The spring gentian is the brilliant blue botanical icon of the Burren and it may be seen in abundance on these hills in spring. The gentian is Alpine in origin and has a remarkably localised distribution in Ireland and the British Isles.

(9) The ruins of a ring fort (Early Christian fortified farmstead) can be picked out 300m beyond the gate on the left (west) of the trail. Two hawthorn trees also stand sentry at this point at either side of the trail. The vista now opening up is quite breathtaking. Galway Bay and the mountains of Connemara act as a spectacular backdrop to the hill of Gleninagh to the northwest while the valleys of Rathborney and Ballyvaughan lie below to the northeast and east respectively.

(10) The trail veers to the left. Stroll on for another 300m to a metal gate. Go through the gate and follow the trail to the right around a sharp elbow. You will come to another metal gate 200m after the elbow. Climb over the conspicuous green-and-yellow metal stile to the right of the gate. Cattle graze these pastures in winter and in so doing fulfil a critical ecological role in keeping

Bloody crane's-bill – a Burren speciality on account of its profusion in the region. Ciarán Ó Riain

The Arctic mountain avens is profuse in the Burren in spring but is otherwise scarce in Ireland and Britain.

down rough grasses and scrub which otherwise would 'choke' the more delicate flora. Yellow-rattle, primrose, tormentil and bloody crane's-bill are just some of the wildflowers thriving on these uplands in spring and summer.

(11) Look out for mountain avens on the left of the trail just after the stile. A plant of the rose family, it is originally from the Arctic Circle and can be classified as a 'very early native' in that it was one of the first wildflowers to colonise the deglaciated landscape in Ireland just over 10,000 years ago. Gragan's Wood to your right is home to a fine canopy of ash. The willow warbler, chiffchaff, blackbird, mistle thrush, song thrush and chaffinch all frequent this habitat. Willow warblers and chiffchaffs breed here but spend the winter in warmer climes.

(12) A 400m descent from the gate and stile will bring you to another sharp elbow. There is a low-sized drystone construction of two short parallel walls at the elbow. This is known as a turf tile. They are quite common in the Burren hills and their function was to dry out fuel such as turf, heathy sods or even cow pats known locally as 'cockbows'. Goldenrod grows on grassy patches here. It is a member of the daisy family and bears tall spikes of small, bright-yellow flowers. Some blackthorn trees also grow on the margins of the trail to the left. The sloes of the blackthorn were once harvested to flavour *poitín*, the illicit potato-based drink.

(13) Continue the descent to a Y-junction and take the sharp right option. Gragan's Wood is now facing you. You will see an extensive area of hazel scrub on the left of the trail. Pass through an old rusty gate.

(14) Encroaching woodland narrows the trail. The woodland floor is habitat to wood sorrel, sanicle and broad-leaved helleborine. Helleborines are orchids that are mainly confined to woodlands in northern temperate regions. Ferns in this area include soft shield fern and golden-scaled male fern. The carnivorous butterwort, the leaves of which resemble a very pale yellowy-green starfish, can also be found at points on the trail which are permanently moistened by the streams of water flowing from the hills. The leaves of the butterwort are slimy in order to trap the insects on which it feeds.

(15) If you look to the left (north) of the trail, you will see a modern livestock shed surrounded by woodland. Ornamental plants, such as fuchsia, Wilson's honey-suckle and common snowberry, are all telltale signs of human habitation in this area and, sure enough, there is an abandoned cottage on the left of the trail. In the past snowberry was planted in gardens for its decorative white fruit. The fruit is poisonous to humans but is part of the diet of pheasants.

Common butterwort consumes insects to supplement its nutrient intake.

(16) Cross over Rathborney River to reach the road. Although this watercourse is commonly referred to as a river, the Ulster Museum palaeontologist Mike Simms more accurately describes it as 'a misfit stream quite out of proportion to the deep valley (Rathborney) it occupies'. Dog rose scrambles extravagantly in the scrub beside the river. Its rosehips are a particularly rich source of vitamin C and provide for an excellent herbal tea. A pair of horse chestnut trees stand guard at either side of the end of the trail. You may turn right at the road to join up with the final 6.5km of the signposted walking route the Burren Way (Route 5, p. 35).

(17) You may now return to the walk starting point by conducting the walk in reverse order.

Ballyvaughan Wood Loop

'King of Tuesday, let live the frail petals in limestone landscapes.'
Seán Dunne, 'Prayer' (1993)

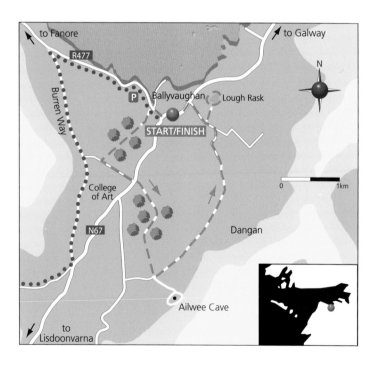

Start/finish: The village of Ballyvaughan on the R477, a one-hour drive north of Ennis. The trailhead is located in the village, at the car park on the coast road to Fanore.

Description: A looped walk featuring some minor roads and unsurfaced tracks. Waymarked with purple arrows.

Highlights: Panoramic views of the great terraces and cliffs of the Burren hills, limestone pavements, Burren wildflowers, ring forts and a brackish lake.

Distance: 8km (5 miles)

Time: 2.5 hours

Grade: Casual

Maps: *The Burren – a map of the uplands of northwest Clare.* Folding Landscapes. Scale: 1:31,680 or OSI *Discovery Series* Map No. 51. Scale: 1:50,000.

(1) Cross the road from the car-parking bay and walk on to the minor road known as the School Road. The National School (1949) is a landmark on the left-hand side after about 0.5km. Walk around the community sports field. Gaelic football is the prime sporting pastime in the north, south and west of County Clare. The east of the county is a hurling stronghold. Just before you reach the clubhouse, the arrow will direct you right. Cross through a stile in the wall.

(2) Cross a small number of fields. These are transformed from pasture to turlough (temporary water body) occasionally. In periods of high rainfall and high tides, the spring water here cannot go underground because of the build-up of seawater below. Thus, the water lodges on the surface and the turlough is formed. Turloughs are almost unique in the world to certain limestone areas in the west and centre of Ireland. This section of the trail may be impassable occasionally.

(3) The landscape soon changes to a patchwork of hazel scrub and limestone pavement. This habitat is an uncommon sight in the otherwise rich pastureland of the Ballyvaughan Valley. Historically, the limestone pavement here would have been interspersed with pockets of pasture for the cattle. However, grazing has been abandoned on account of its marginal economic value and so the opportunistic hazel has established itself. However, keep an eye out for the odd ash tree towering above the hazel. A hazel/ash woodland is inevitable with time.

Limestone pavement has been exposed due to glacial action and unsustainable prehistoric farming.

(4) Having emerged from the scrub, cross just one more field. The cylindrical Newtown castle is to the southwest. The castle has been magnificently restored and is part of the complex of buildings which make up the Burren College of Art (1993). The castle was one of the power seats of the O'Lochlann kingdom in medieval times.

Exit the field by a stile which brings you on to a minor road. Turn left and you soon arrive at a junction which merges with the busy N67 road. Turn left here and immediately turn right on to another minor road. This road eventually gives way to an unsurfaced track. You then arrive at a metal gate. Cross the stile here and turn left immediately. The bright canopy above the entrance to Ailwee Cave is visible in the slopes of Ailwee Hill (286m) straight ahead. You are now walking on a track across pasture which is used as winter grazing for the cattle.

(5) This cross-country section ends at a minor road which leads to the Ailwee Cave. The Burren show cave was formerly known as McGann's Cave, after the local man Jack McGann who discovered it in 1944. The cave system consists of a kilometre of underground passages leading in to the core of Ailwee Hill. Pass by the cave entrance.

(6) A kilometre further on, you will notice a circular clump of trees in a field to the left. The trees are, in fact, growing over the stone fort of Cathair na hUamhain (the fort of the cave). There are no fewer than five such ring forts in a couple of square miles in this immediate area. This concentration of fortified first-millennium farmsteads is testament to the excellence of the farming land hereabouts. The fields you pass by are known as improved grasslands. Farming in the Burren lowlands in general has become far more specific and intense since Ireland's accession to the EU (formerly EEC) in 1973.

(7) You will spot some drystone walls made from large rocks. These walls have been constructed mechanically rather than by hand and are a sign of the land clearances of the last couple of decades. A local wag has christened these boundaries 'Weetabix' walls on account of their likeness to the well-known breakfast cereal.

Cappanawalla (312m) with Galway Bay and Connemara in the background. Eimer Ni Riain

This section of the trail illustrates the strong contrast between the topography of the Burren lowlands and uplands. The rare global landform of limestone pavement can be seen at altitude whereas in the lowlands at either side of this minor road, the conventional Irish topography of improved grasslands is evident. The lowlands are home to the economically more productive agriculture. However, the uplands are far richer in terms of natural and cultural heritage.

(8) Cappanawalla Hill (312m) is off to the left of the trail and Ailwee Hill is to the right. The place name Ailwee comes from the Irish *Aill Bhuí*, meaning 'yellow cliff'. Although gorse is most uncommon in the Burren, it is widespread on the limestone pavement area to the left as you progress. The shrub blooms from February to May and the profusion of yellow flowers can be quite a spectacle. However, even though it is a native shrub, gorse can upset the ecological balance. The dense thickets in this area outcompete the more delicate Burren wildflowers which would otherwise thrive on the limestone pavement.

(9) The trail changes from minor road to unsurfaced track, known as a green road. In the Burren, these are ancient cattle highways of indeterminate age. Some of the tracks are occasionally still used for this purpose. However, they are more commonly used now by walkers. When you pass through the metal gate known as Dangan Gate, the trail veers left.

The spring gentian with its brilliant blue flowers is an icon of the Burren. Emma Glanville

63

(10) Stroll on 0.75km from Dangan Gate to a T-junction. Turn left here and then right at the next junction for a short, wonderful detour to the shores of the serene Lough Rask. The water level of the lake can fluctuate wildly, being influenced heavily by tides and rainfall – just like the turlough at the start of the trail. The lake is actually connected to the sea by an underground channel and thus Lough Rask is neither saline nor freshwater but a mixture of both, i.e. brackish.

In winter the open water is frequented by tigeon and weal, while the rush beds give shelter to moorhens. A breeding colony of grey herons nests in the trees near the lake.

When the weather is rough in Galway Bay, little egrets retreat inland for shelter to places like Lough Rask where they can also enjoy still backwaters to feed in. It is an African bird which started breeding in Ireland only in 1997. As the globe gets warmer, more and more little egrets are seeking cooler climes in the north of the world.

(11) Return to the junction and turn right. About 350m further on there is a gateway on the right which leads to Ballyvaughan Church of Ireland cemetery. The Church of Ireland community in north Clare is tiny and this explains why there is such a small number of headstones in evidence here. The site is an oasis of calm. There had been a church here up to the 1940s. However, the building was dismantled stone by stone and transported to the Burren village of Noughaval. The present Roman Catholic church in Noughaval was built with the transposed materials.

(12) You soon arrive at a T-Junction. Turn left here along the main road (N67). Use the footpath where available or alternatively walk facing oncoming traffic. Within a few minutes you will have returned via Ballyvaughan to the trailhead on the coast road to Fanore.

ROUTE 10:
Carran Turlough

'Beauty is everlasting
And its worship can never be out of season.'
Robert Lloyd Praeger, *The Way That I Went* (1937)

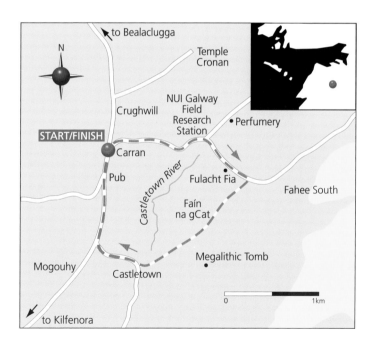

Start/finish: Carran village. From Corrofin, follow the R476 heading towards Kilfenora/Lisdoonvarna. Turn right onto the R480 at Leamaneh Castle. Take the second turn right for Carran village.

Description: The walk is along a surfaced road. It consists of a short loop around the largest turlough in the region. Most of the road is very tranquil.

Highlights: Wildfowl, a ring fort, a medieval castle, a *fulacht fia* (prehistoric burnt mound), a herdsman's cottage and much local history and folklore. Burren wildflowers in spring. The walk is both pram- and wheelchair-friendly.

Distance: 5km (3 miles)

Time: 1.5 hours

Grade: Casual

Maps: *The Burren – a map of the uplands of northwest Clare.* Folding Landscapes. Scale: 1:31,680 or OSI *Discovery Series* Map No. 51. Scale: 1:50,000.

(1) The walk begins at the car park outside Cassidy's pub. The car park offers great views of the Carran polje, which is a flat-floored depression hollowed out by the dissolution of rock by rainwater. Poljes are also characterised by steep enclosing flanks. The 7km^2 floor of the Carran polje is covered with glacial sediment making for fertile land. The pasture is highly regarded even though cattle can graze it only on a seasonal basis.

Some of the flanks of the polje have vertical bands of boulder clay running down them. This amalgam of clay, stone and boulders was deposited by melting glaciers. Swallow holes in the polje floor drain away surface water into the underground water channels. However, these channels are unable to draw down all surface water in periods of high rainfall and thus a temporary lake or turlough is formed on the surface. When the turlough waters disappear underground they wash the grasslands with calcium, which enhances the bone structure of the cattle that graze here. The Carran turlough in full flood covers 1.5km^2 of the polje floor and is the largest turlough in the region.

(2) With your back to the pub, turn right and walk down the village street. A nineteenth-century schoolhouse is on the right at the end of the street. A tablet on the building states that the founder of the Gaelic Athletic Association (GAA), Michael Cusack, taught here. Cusack, born near

Carran turlough, the Burren's largest seasonal lake. Emma Glanville

Carran, described the GAA as being 'for the preservation and cultivation of the national pastimes of Ireland'. The GAA was nationalist in its political outlook and was an integral part of the broader late nineteenth- and early twentieth-century movement which fought successfully for self-government for Ireland.

(3) Turn right just after the old schoolhouse. You will almost immediately pass the current national school on your right. The National University of Ireland (NUI) Galway Field Research Station (opened in 1975) is on the left a little further on. The station provides accommodation for visiting students and academic staff.

You come to a junction soon after the research station. Ireland's oldest working perfumery, The Burren Perfumery, is a few hundred metres along the road to the left. It is set in secluded woodland and is also home to an excellent organic cafe. However, you continue straight on.

(4) Half a kilometre beyond the perfumery junction is the upright of a former signpost on the right-hand side. The sign has long since disappeared but the post remains. It formerly indicated a *fulacht fia* ('cooking site of the deer') in the field to the right. When you enter the field you will see the horseshoe-shaped mound. A trough, usually made of oak, was placed in a hollow in the ground. The trough was filled with water from a nearby source (in this case the Carran turlough). Stones were heated by fire and then placed in the trough. In this way, up to 450 litres of

water could reach boiling point in 30 minutes. The boiling water may then have been used to carry out several different functions, including cooking and hide processing. When the stones were so fragmented that they were no longer of use, they were discarded around the trough, creating a small, distinct U-shaped landform. This mound was excavated in the 1980s. Findings included animal bone, burnt stones and the remains of the oak trough. *Fulachtaí fia* have been dated to the Bronze Age. This field is very rich in Burren flora in spring.

(5) The ruins of a herdsman's cottage are a couple of hundred metres beyond the *fulacht fia* on the same side of the road. Herdsmen were keepers of the cattle in the Burren uplands in winter on behalf of large rancher farmers. The herdsman received use of a house and garden and also some free grazing in return for herding. This cottage was reduced to its present state of ruin by an accidental fire. You can see from the stonework that this cottage was extended during its lifetime (hersdmen's cottages are usually smaller in size).

(6) Take the right-hand turn just after the ruin and begin the walk along the eastern side of the turlough. There is a depression on the right between the road and the polje floor: it is a doline, i.e. a funnel-shaped hollow formed by the erosion of rock by rainwater. The local place name for the doline area is *Fána na gCat* ('the cats' slope'), as it was an assembly point for feral cats in the past.

(7) The turlough is frequented in winter by wildfowl such as wigeon, teal and white-fronted geese. White-fronted geese spend the summer in Greenland, and have an orange bill and legs. The Gulf Stream ensures that Ireland's temperatures seldom drop below zero in winter and so our lakes and rivers rarely freeze, which attracts such winter visitors.

(8) About 1.5km along the eastern side of the polje is the Early Christian fort of Cahersavaun, a couple of hundred metres to the right of the road. It is surrounded in winter by the turlough, which would have been a welcome extra defensive feature. Forts such as Cahersavaun protected the occupants from attack by rival clans and wolves that preyed on sheep and cattle. Dairy, beef and sheep farming were carried out at farmsteads such as this in Early Christian times. Farming in the polje and in the wider Burren now focuses mainly on beef cattle rearing.

(9) You soon come to a T-junction. Turn right here. On the right of the road is a castle, 100m beyond the junction. This castle or tower house was one of the many medieval strongholds of the O'Lochlann family. Ireland consisted of a series of petty kingdoms in medieval times as it had yet to establish a nation state with a centralised power structure. The royalty of the O'Lochlann family is represented on the castle's northern side by a carved head with a crown. A second carved head is missing, having disappeared in unclear circumstances some years ago. The ruined state of the castle is a telling reminder of how the reign of the Gaelic aristocracy in

the west of Ireland ended in the mid-1600s during the Cromwellian period. (10) The field on the right, 100m beyond the castle, is known locally as 'the bull field', with boulders spread evenly around it. The former landowner kept a bull in the field. If it became aggressive, the farmer felt he would be safe from attack by seeking refuge atop the nearest boulder. The hill due north of here is Termon (243 m), which is featured in Route 2 (p. 13).

(11) You arrive at a T-junction. Turn right here and make the short walk uphill to the village. Please face oncoming traffic as the road can be quite busy. You arrive back at the pub car park at the top of the hill.

A local man told me that there were often reports in the past of a phosphorescent light seen hovering in the turlough at night. The light was believed to be a will-o'-the-wisp. At best, it was considered to be a nuisance designed to confuse the traveller; at worst, the light was feared as a supernatural force to be avoided at all costs. If your walk finishes in darkness and you spot the will-o'-the-wisp, my only advice is to repair to the pub!

ROUTE 11:
Dromore Wood

'I built my house in a forest far from the venal roar,
Somebody please beat a path to my door.'
Derek Mahon, 'Light Music' (1977)

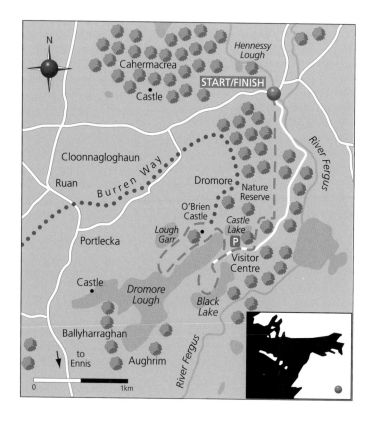

Start/finish: Near Ruan village. From Ennis, take the N18 in the Galway direction for 3km. When you see the Ennis Supply Company on the left, turn left and drive straight on for 7km until you reach Ruan. Dromore Wood is on the right as you approach. However, in order to reach the entrance point of the wood, turn right in Ruan as signposted and then take the next turn right at the 400m mark outside the village. Continue for another 2.5km to reach the entrance, which is on the right-hand side of the road. There is ample car parking space at the entrance area.

Description: The walk is of an amalgam of three trails. The first goes from the reserve entrance to the information centre (this trail was not waymarked at the time of writing). The walk also includes two waymarked trails: the Castle Trail and the Rabbit Island Trail. The final leg of the walk is the return along the trail from the information centre to the entrance.

Highlights: A peaceful, leisurely stroll in a magnificent and extensive native woodland bordered by the River Fergus and five lakes.

Distance: 9km (5.6 miles)

Time: 3 hours

Grade: Casual

Map and Booklet: *The Castle Trail and Rabbit Island Trail Walks, Dromore Wood Nature Reserve.* Nick Parry. Published by Office of Public Works. On sale at the information centre which is open each year from mid-May to September. www.npws.ie

Author's note: A nature reserve is a protective designation given in law to an area that is considered to be of national importance on account of either its wildlife diversity or its geological heritage. There are approximately eighty nature reserves in the Republic of Ireland.

Dromore Wood received National Nature Reserve designation in 1985 on account of its wildlife importance. The reserve is about 400 hectares in size and boasts a wide variety of habitats including lakes, rivers, turloughs, fens, callows (flooded meadows), limestone pavement, reed beds and woodland.

Trail A: Main Entrance to Information Centre/ Car Park – 2km (1.25 miles)

(1) Enter the reserve through the first gate. The River Fergus is on your left-hand side. All the lakes in Dromore Wood drain into the Fergus, which rises in the Burren in north Clare and goes through seven lakes before reaching Ennis. It eventually joins the Shannon's tidal waters in the east Clare village of Newmarket-on-Fergus.

Stoats are solitary animals and they thrive in the scrub-covered areas of the Burren.

Pass through the second gate, which has a cattle grid. You will see a track on the right after 20m. Leave the road at this point and walk along the track into a thinly wooded area of ash, beech and silver birch. You are only a couple of hundred metres from your car and are already in sylvan wonderland! Walk through the woodland floor here for 25m approximately and then you will clearly see an old, wide track on the left. Proceed along this track, which has decayed drystone walls visible on its left-hand side. The trail is used now only for recreational purposes but originally it was the old entrance road into the Dromore demesne. The woodland floor is rich in ferns and mosses. These primitive plant families really appreciate damp habitats like this – sheltered from the drying effect of wind.

(2) Continue along the track for about 400m and you come to a T-junction. Turn left here and continue for about 25m until you see another track on the right. Turn into this track. There are plenty of ash, hawthorn and Norway spruce on either side of the trail, and some felled trees are evident also. The wood management plan is to phase out gradually the alien species of Norway spruce, sycamore and beech and thus facilitate the natural regeneration of our native hardwood trees. You will pass an impressive moss-covered erratic on the left of the track. The dominant trees in this area are ash and hazel (which are often found in association with each other). The nuts

One of the highest concentrations of pine martens in the world is to be found at Dromore Wood.

of the hazel are a good source of protein for the red squirrels in the wood. (3) At the next T-junction, there is a stile of stone steps almost immediately to your right at the far side of the intersection. Go through this stile. You will soon cross over a decayed drystone wall and walk through a gap in another wall ruin. Continue along

Guelder-rose favours damp, lime-rich soil.

this track until you come to the next T-junction. Turn right here. You pass a timber shed on the left, a disused forestry shed. The Forestry Division of the state managed the wood from the 1940s until 1985 when responsibility passed to the NPWS. Walk a further 200m, then go through a significant opening on your left onto a track, which soon becomes wider. Decayed drystone walls define the margins of the track. Cuckoo pint, or lords and ladies, thrives on the floor of the woodland hereabouts. This wildflower loves shady places and its berries are orange-red in colour and are poisonous. Flora in Dromore is quite typical of calcareous woodlands and also includes common milkwort, herb Robert, primrose, lesser celandine, honeysuckle, dog rose and bluebell.

(4) As you progress, note the ivy carpeting the ground and climbing the trees. Ivy contributes significantly to the biodiversity of the wood as its berries are an important food source for birds, pine martens and badgers. It also provides valuable shelter for nesting birds. The final junction soon presents itself in the form of a 'crossroad'. Go straight through here and walk along this last short leg of the track until you reach the entrance road of the reserve.

(5) Turn right here and walk the short distance to the car park and information centre which are on the right-hand side of the road. A speed limit for cars of 25km/h operates in the reserve, with speed ramps to help enforce the limit. Small lay-bys have been cut into the woodland margins to allow vehicles to pass each other. The information centre is open for three months each summer and distributes information and materials regarding the walking trails and the heritage of the wood. There is also an information display board in the car park. Toilet facilities are open all year round.

Trail B: The Castle Trail – 3km (1.9 miles)

(1) Take the Castle Trail exit (signposted) from the car park. Walk across the wooden deck, which was built in 2006 over a causeway between Dromore (left) and Castle Lough (right). The deck is not level as it undulates with the contours of the causeway, which was once a defensive feature of Dromore Castle.

(2) Dromore Castle is on your left after the causeway, one of many castles built between the 1400s and the 1600s by the powerful, extended clan of O'Briens who dominated the kingdom of Thomond in medieval times. (Thomond corresponds to the modern county of Clare.) The castle is now in ruins but must have been a most impressive edifice, surrounded on three sides by water. What is left of the interior can be glimpsed by going around the back to the lakeside. Though the castle has long since been abandoned by humans, there are still a couple of castle residents in the form of pipistrelles (Ireland's most abundant bat). There is also a colony of lesser horseshoe bats roosting in another old building in the wood. The lesser horseshoe is of international importance and Ireland has the largest population of this bat species in Europe.

(3) You come to a junction after 30m. Turn left here to follow the Castle Trail as signposted.

(4) You will soon come to a wooden seat on the left-hand side of the trail. This stop serves as a viewing point for the lake and castle. However, the view is being gradually diminished by the rise of sycamores and hazels between the seat and the lake.

(5) You will next meet the first fork in the trail. Go left. The limestone boulder beside the next wooden seat has been heavily dimpled due to erosion by rainwater. There is Norway spruce behind the seat and guelder-rose opposite it.

(6) Continue along the track until you come to another wooden seat. Note the very tall brackens on the right of the seat, which are reaching skywards to ensure that the trees do not entirely occlude the light from them. As you progress, you can see the sword-shaped leaves and showy flowers of the yellow iris on your left-hand side. Yellow iris is one of our prettiest wildflowers and loves damp habitats like this lake edge. Remnants of a drystone wall are a little further on again, on the left. Go left at the next fork, thus keeping close to the lake. You will very soon have the chance to stand on limestone right on the edge of the lake. There is a sudden, deep drop to the bottom of the lake. Dromore Castle is barely visible off to your left. Flowers growing in this immediate area include devil's-bit scabious, bramble, St John's Wort and meadowsweet.

(7) You are walking very near the lake edge and the track opens out from the woodland into a small area of grassland with some limestone protrusions. On the damp, lime-rich soil to the left, you will find willow,

purging buckthorn and guelder-rose, while ash, hazel and birch dominate to your right. Birch is often found at the margins of lakes and rivers. Its leaf litter plays an important ecological role as it nourishes the soil and makes it rich enough for other trees, such as oak, to establish themselves. Just after this grassland area, you will see the only stone seat

Devil's-bit scabious and oxeye daisy

on the Castle Trail. Look down south from this vantage point to view the wide expanse of Dromore Lake and its heavily wooded margins. This view gives you an excellent idea of what most of Ireland looked like prior to the arrival of the Stone Age farmers with their polished axes and deforestation schemes 6,000 years ago.

(8) The track now returns to an area of thick woodland where the joyous sight of young oak trees awaits. The oak is our largest tree and can live for up to 1,000 years. It is an extremely rich source of folklore because of its size and long lifespan. The woodland on the left eventually clears to give fine views of the farmlands that separate Dromore Lake and Lough Garr. The track veers right and the next landmark is a truly majestic, mature ash tree growing expansively in a unconfined environment. It is to the right of the track at a bend. Lough Garr is on the left as you continue and there is a wooden bench with a lake vista on the right of the track. Lough Garr's waters have a high calcium content – just like those of the other four lakes in the catchment of the River Fergus in Dromore Wood – which assists in the healthy growth of fish and plant communities in the lakes.

(9) You will soon pass an erratic, 2m in height, on the left of the trail. Keep an eye out for a Scots pine. It is growing just a couple of metres beyond the next wooden seat on the left of the track. Scots pine is arguably our only native pine, although it disappeared altogether from Ireland about 2,000 years ago – possibly due to climatic factors. It was reintroduced over the last couple of hundred years and all the Scots pine now in Ireland derive from seeds or plants from elsewhere. You will also pass an enormous tree trunk on the left of the path, the remains of a 200-year-old beech tree felled by a great storm in 2001. The trunk serves as an ideal habitat for certain lichens.

(10) The last wooden seat on this trail is up ahead on the left. A couple of disused badger setts are visible on the right just beyond the seat. Apart from badgers, you may have the good fortune to see other wild animals such as pine martens, red squirrels, foxes, otters and hares in the reserve.

Dromore Wood is reckoned to have the highest concentration of pine martens in the world. The dense cover and huge variety of berries in the wood are much appreciated by these arboreal carnivores. There is a slight ascent along the track from here to a small cluster of mature beech trees. Just gaze heavenwards and marvel at their height! Beech can grow to 40m. It is not native to Ireland, having been introduced via the Anglo-Irish estates in the eighteenth and nineteenth centuries. The beech trees in this area are estimated to be about 150 years old. As they are non-native, they will eventually be felled by the NPWS to make way for a new generation of native tree species. You next come to a bend in the trail where there is a signpost for the car park. As you progress, the track goes through an old estate wall. The building on your right is the ruin of the O'Brien chapel, which is contemporaneous with the castle. Proceed to the next junction and go straight through it in order to return to base at the car park.

Trail C: Rabbit Island Trail – 2km (1.25 miles)

(1) The trail is so called as there was a large rabbit population here prior to the change of habitat from short grass pasture to woodlands. Take the Rabbit Island Trail (signposted) from the car park. Go over the footbridge, which crosses the stretch of water linking the Black Lake on the left with Dromore Lake on the right. There is a slipway for private fishing boats at either side of the bridge. The lakes are excellent angling waters for salmon, trout and many other coarse fish.

Water-tolerant willow is profuse at the lake edges. The air is alive with birdsong. The woodland is home to finches, blue tits and willow warblers. Birds of prey include the buzzard and kestrel. Though the long-eared owl has not yet been recorded, it is probably a resident as it likes to nest in damp woodland. The damp, lime-rich habitat just after the bridge is a haven for guelder-rose and buckthorn. Guelder-rose is actually a member of the honeysuckle family while buckthorn is Ireland's rarest native tree.

(2) You will come to a tiny lay-by on the left of the path. You may spot some felled Norway spruce here. The felling is to facilitate the natural regeneration of our native ash in the space vacated by the spruce. The next landmark is a stone seat on your left, which affords partial views of Dromore Lake. Tall willows are now increasingly limiting the lake vista here.

(3) Just 20m further on to your left, young and vigorous sycamores have established themselves. Though sycamore is not native to Ireland, it is prolific here. These sycamores will also be felled in time.

(4) You next round a corner of the path, veering left and east towards Black Lake. You will spot some Norway spruce with its needles and cones on the left. If it seems familiar, it is because its greatest claim to fame is its use as the Christmas tree.

(5) There are two minor tracks off the trail on your right. Take the second track and arrive at a limestone table and seats. This little picnic area is dedicated to Johnny O'Donoghue who worked in the reserve as a general operative for over forty years. A sketch of a pine marten accompanies the dedication to Johnny on the table.

Spindle in its autumn splendour.

The extensive reed beds on the margins of the lake provide shelter for many waterfowl species. The roots of the reeds are a valuable food source for swans. In spring, the coot makes its nest with the reeds. Winter migrants include ducks such as wigeon, teal, shoveler, pintail and tufted duck. The grey heron can often be seen in shallow water by the reeds. There is also a pair of great crested grebes on the lake. This is a sublime place to just sit and listen to the symphony of birdsong.

(6) Evidence of glacial deposition is provided by the great limestone boulders on the edge of the trail. The woodland floor is carpeted with bramble, hart's-tongue fern and ivy. Felled Norway spruce is strewn in the woodland on your left while there are mature hazel trees beyond the spruce on the opposite side of the path. Hazel has a lifespan of about eighty years; however, coppicing (the cutting back of trees to ground level to stimulate their growth) can double its life.

(7) The next landmark is another limestone seat, on the left of the path, with a lake view. The seat is overhung with hazel and spindle. Spindle is inconspicuous for most of the year. In autumn, however, it becomes a spectacle of crimson leaves and fruits. As you approach a junction, the path is bordered on either side by young, tall ash trees, which are constantly seeking altitude and light in this confined woodland space. Take the right turn at the junction and cross the footbridge again to return to the car park.

Trail D: Return to Information Centre/Car Park to Main Entrance – 2km (1.25 miles)

'A' above in reverse.

ROUTE 12:
Coole Park

*'The bell-beat of their wings above my head
Trod with a lighter tread.'*
W. B. Yeats, 'The Wild Swans at Coole' (1919)

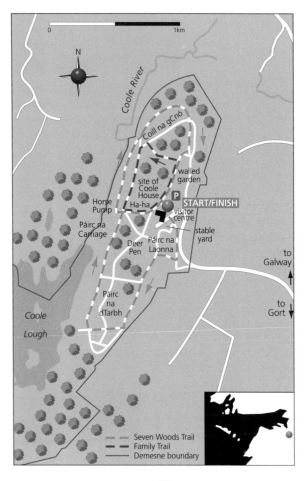

Start/finish: Coole Park Visitor Centre, Gort, County Galway. Coole Park is just off the N18, 3km northwest of Gort.

Description: Two waymarked nature trails within an excellently managed Nature Reserve.

Highlights: A walled garden, an ancient native woodland and the Coole watercourse including a lake, a river and a turlough.

Distance 6.25km (4 miles)

Time: 2.5 hours

Grade: Casual

Map: *The Family Trail* and *The Seven Woods Trail* Booklet and Map, on sale at the visitor centre. www.coolepark.ie. Tel. 091 631 804.

Author's note: Robert Gregory bought Coole Estate in the mid-1700s. In 1880, his great-grandson, Sir William Gregory, former Governor of Ceylon, married a fellow member of the aristocratic elite, Augusta Persse, who then became Lady Gregory, mistress of Coole Park. Lady Gregory was a dramatist and folklorist. Her closest collaborator was the poet William Butler Yeats. Coole Park was Yeats' summer retreat for several years. Gregory, Yeats and Sir Edward Martyn of nearby Tullira Castle established the new Irish Literary Theatre, later to become the Abbey Theatre.

The state bought the estate in 1927 and the Forestry Service managed it until 1987. Since then, the estate and the adjacent Garryland Wood have been in the care of the NPWS.

Coole and Garryland Nature Reserve are very rich in natural heritage and comprise 405 hectares of woodlands, wetlands and limestone pavement.

Family Trail: follow the red-lettered stops along trail – 1.5km (1 mile)

The walk begins and ends at the visitor centre.

(a) Site of Coole House

With your back to the visitor centre, turn left. Pass the Deer Pen on your left. The trail veers right.

Coole Park nature trail in autumn

On the left-hand side of the trail is the site of the former house of the Gregorys. It was built by Robert Gregory in 1770. You can see a photograph of the former house in a display board to the northeast of it. The house, built along simple, symmetrical lines, was the centre of the Irish Literary Revival in the early twentieth century. The dining room and drawing room were to the rear of the house and enjoyed fine vistas of Coole Lough and the Burren hills.

The house was in a state of decay when the Forestry Service took over the estate in the twentieth century, who unfortunately demolished it in 1941. The Forestry Service plantations to the rear of the site mean that one can no longer view the lake and the Burren hills from this point.

(b) The Walled Garden

Enter the walled garden. It is 1.8 hectares in area. A young Indian bean tree is on the left of the path. The tree is native to North America and Asia and is cultivated in Europe as an ornamental. Its flower is white with yellow and purple spots. Lady Gregory's favourite refuge in the estate was in the shade of a previous *Catalpa*. This one was planted by her granddaughters (see wall plaque).

The marble bust of Maecenas in the walled garden.

There is a marble bust of Maecenas at the opposite side of the garden to the bean tree. Maecenas, who lived in the first century BC, was a Roman statesman and patron of poets such as Virgil and Horace.

There is a row of yew trees in the garden between the bean tree and the bust. They are readily identifiable as cultivars rather than the wild variety on account of their straight aspect. Some of the fruits and vegetables for Coole House were grown in hothouses in the walled garden. The ruins of the hothouses can be seen beside the yew trees.

The path is bordered on both sides by box, a European evergreen shrub with a hard, heavy timber. It is widely used for hedging. The copper beech on your right as you progress is the famous 'autograph tree', in the bark of which Lady Gregory's literary guests carved their initials. A plaque alongside the tree explains which writer is represented by each set of initials. Included are William and Jack Butler Yeats, George Bernard Shaw, John Masefield and Sean O'Casey.

Coole Park. The autograph tree (a copper beech) bears the initials of many famous writers on its bark.

(c) Lime Tree

You leave the walled garden through a gap on the left of the path. Turn left as indicated soon after leaving the garden. The mature tree a couple of metres left of stop C is a lime tree. The entrance avenue of Coole Estate is also lined with limes. All the trees were planted near the house and gardens by the Gregorys in the middle of the nineteenth century. Our streets and avenues were often decorated with lime trees in the past but they have now been replaced by more fungus- and insect-resistant tree species.

Through an old gateway ahead, you enter an area called Coill na gCnó ('the nut wood'). Yeats immortalised this wood through his poem 'To a squirrel at Kyle-Na-No' (Kyle-Na-No is an anglicisation of the place name).

(d) Coole River

When you come to a bend, turn left and start walking in a southerly direction. You are now strolling parallel to Coole River, which has its source in the Slieve Aughty Mountains to the east and flows into the sea at

Kinvarra to the west. The river disappears under the limestone surface on several occasions on its journey from mountain to sea.

The dominant tree in this area is beech. It is native to some woodlands in the south of England but otherwise is an exotic species in Great Britain and Ireland. The floor of the beech wood includes beech saplings, holly, ferns and cherry laurel. A Himalayan native, Cherry laurel has evergreen leaves and was initially planted here in estate times. It is classified as an invasive alien in Ireland.

(e) Bats

Stop E is beside a beech tree. A bat box placed on this tree makes an excellent roosting site for one of the most threatened mammal types in Ireland. Eight of our nine native bats are to be found at Coole. Bats are the second most diverse order of mammals in the world after rodents. There are 970 living species of bats that we know of. Bats in Ireland live on a diet of insects and forage for them after dark.

(f) The Horse Pump and Coole Lough

The circular feature at the edge of the turlough is the site of the horse pump. A horse tied to a timber shaft walked in a circle and thus created the horsepower that enabled a suction pump to draw water from the lake. The water was then conducted by an underground pipe from this site to Coole House.

The turlough is usually flooded in winter and almost completely dried out in summer. Turloughs only form in areas of high rainfall and in pure bedded limestone. These limestone areas are very calcareous and also have well developed joint systems that water can readily attack and permeate, which is why turloughs are concentrated almost exclusively in the west and the centre of Ireland. The only recorded turlough outside Ireland is in North Wales.

One of Ireland's rarest native trees, purging buckthorn, thrives here on the turlough margins. It grows only on damp, lime-rich soil.

(g) Back Lawn and Ha-ha

The back lawn was a large open field of 6.5 hectares in Gregory estate times. The Forestry Service subsequently planted the lawn with the exotic conifers you see today. However, the long-term plan is to remove the exotica and replace them with native trees.

The man-made ditch on your left is a 'ha-ha', i.e. a ditch with a wall on its inner side below ground level, forming a boundary to a park or garden without interrupting the view. In this case, the ditch was built as a boundary in the back lawn to ensure that the view of the lake and the Burren hills from Coole House was not compromised.

(h) The Deer Pen

The pen was formerly an old orchard and vegetable garden less than 1 hectare in size. The garden has served as a deer pen since 1971 when red deer were brought to Coole from Killarney National Park. The red deer is classified as a 'late native' as it was introduced to Ireland in Late Stone Age/Early Bronze Age times from the Bay of Biscay. Other late natives include the goat, badger, pine marten and red squirrel. There are only a few thousand red deer left in Ireland now owing to destruction of their woodland habitat. They are largely confined to the northern and western counties. The deer's diet includes grasses as well as the leaves from oak, holly, ivy and heather. Deer also like woody shoots, which is why the apple trees in the pen are protected from browsing. Ireland's other two deer species are fallow deer, which was introduced by the Normans in medieval times, and sika deer, introduced in the nineteenth century.

If you face the pen, the visitor centre is about 25m to your left along the path.

Seven Woods Trail: follow the blue-numbered stops along the trail – 4.5km (2.8 miles)

The walk begins and ends at the visitor centre.

(1) The Stable Yard

With your back to the entrance door to the visitor centre, turn right and walk about 25 m. The old stable yard of Coole Estate is on your right. The ruins of the coach house are on the left of the yard. A shelter with nest holes (i.e. dovecotes) for domesticated pigeons was created here in the 1700s by indenting the walls. Robert Gregory commissioned this piece of work so that the pigeons could provide meat and eggs during the winter when fresh meat was scarce. This indented dovecote is one of the few surviving examples in the west of Ireland.

(2) The Lime Kiln

This part of the Coole farm was known as Páirc na Laonna ('the calves' field'). The drystone construction is a limekiln. The kilns were used to make fertiliser from limestone by first burning it, then adding watered lime and finally adding water. The end product made for an excellent fertiliser with a tiny carbon footprint. The kilns fell into disuse during the 1800s as imported fertilisers became more popular. The size of the kiln and its relative sophistication are indicators of the prosperity of the landowners.

(3) Páirc na dTarbh

Páirc na dTarbh is translated as 'the bulls' field'. As the name suggests, this area was once part of the Coole farmlands of the Gregorys. When the Forestry Service took over the management of Coole, they planted conifers here, some of which can still be seen on the right of the trail. The conifers, mostly Norway Spruce, are of little ecological value. These alien softwoods were planted for short-term economic gain as they mature far more quickly than our own native hardwoods. The conifers, which were on the left of the trail, have been removed as part of the Coole Park conservation programme. They have been replaced by young broadleaf trees such as ash and hazel.

The mature tree beside stop 3 is an ash. A tall, mature ash such as this is a symbol of the well-being of the land. The ash can grow to a height of 45m and survive for 200 years.

(4) Birds

Many of the common birds of the countryside are present in the Coole Park woods, including wood pigeon, blackbird, robin, song thrush, wren, chaffinch, blue tit, coal tit, great tit and long-tailed tit. These birds also frequent hedgerows, scrub and gardens in the countryside. The treecreeper and the jay are much less common in the countryside and frequent only extensive areas of woodland such as this. Chiffchaffs, willow warblers and blackcaps are all summer visitors. The uncommon long-eared owl nests at Coole. It is a ground-nesting bird but may also nest in old crow or magpie nests and disused squirrel dreys.

(5) Woodland Plants

March and April are the best flowering months in Coole. The trees will be in leaf later in the year and then most of the woodland wildflowers will be deprived of the precious light they need in order to bloom. Wood sorrel, wild garlic, wood violet, primrose, wood anemone and bluebell are all part of the multicoloured mosaic in spring. The bluebell is a member of the lily family and is one of the glories of Coole. Its lavender-blue flowers are pendulous, bell-shaped and slightly fragrant. The honey-coloured bird's-nest orchid also abounds in the beech woods.

(6) Oak and Yew

This area is known as Inchy Wood from the Irish *Coill na hInse* meaning 'river meadow wood'. These southern and western areas of Coole remained largely intact during both the Gregory and Forestry Service eras. The native woodlands trace their descent from prehistoric times. The tree on the left of the stop is a pedunculate oak. Our other oak type is sessile and is found on acidic soils. Oak woodland is very rich in animal and plant life.

The tree 20m to the right of the stop is a yew, and bears a metal identification plate on its bark. It is interesting to contrast the sinuous form of this wild yew with the upright shape of the planted yews in the walled garden. Yew is a common cultivar in cemeteries because of its powerful symbolism: its poisonous evergreen leaves represent death, its tough timber symbolises the afterlife whilst its long lifespan associates it with eternity.

(7) Coole Lough

There are sweeping views across the lake westwards to the northeast of the Burren region. Many of the Burren hills that you can see are distinguished by great prehistoric burial mounds on their summits. A Scots pine, with a helpful metal identification plate on its bark, is at this stop. Its conifer seeds are one of the favourite foods of the red squirrel.

(8) Red Squirrel

The beautiful inhabitant of the tree canopy at Coole is the Eurasian red squirrel. It is a joy to see it move with dexterity from branch to branch. It uses its tail for both balance and steering. The red squirrel population is declining in Europe due to the continued advance of its more robust relative, the North American grey squirrel. Though the latter continues to advance westwards across Ireland, it has still not reached west of the Shannon river.

Laurel was introduced to Europe from the Himalayas as a garden ornamental tree. However, it has spread and has had a negative impact ecologically, as it shades the seedlings of our native trees in Coole Park. There is only a little laurel now left in this area of the park thanks to the conservation work of the NPWS.

The red squirrel's diet includes acorns, nuts, berries and fungi.

(9) Drystone Walls

You are now entering Páirc na Carraige ('the rock field'). A pair of double drystone walls leads from the farmyard and the lower fields (now woodland) to the turlough. When Robert Gregory acquired the estate in the 1700s, he commissioned a great drystone wall-building programme. This pair of double walls served as a cattle highway. The cattle were transferred in the summer from the lower fields to the dried-out turlough area, which served as excellent summer pasture. This movement of cattle was, in essence, a highly localised form of transhumance within the estate. Double walls such as this one are usually found on very good land.

(10) Birch

Silver birch grows on the edges of bogs, rivers and lakes. It is often planted in gardens and towns as an ornamental. The nest-like structures you see on the birch treetops are abnormal growths of weak shoots caused by fungal attack. The fungus is known as *Taphrina betulina* or 'birch witches' brooms' and can be caused by currents of water or air. It is often also caused by mite infestation in warm summer weather.

(11) The Horse Pump and Coole Lough

The Horse Pump and Coole Lough are described at (f) in the description of the Family Trail on p. 82.

(12) Pine Martens and Beech

This area is known as An Choill Dorcha, ('the dark wood'). This wood was burnt down at the end of the nineteenth century and was subsequently replanted with beech trees. Beech is not native to Ireland and now, as part of a conservation programme, it is being cut down and replaced by native species. This area is frequented by Ireland's most beautiful mammal, the pine marten. Its droppings can be readily spotted on top of the drystone walls hereabouts. The pine marten is associated with woodland and scrub across Europe. Higher densities are found in areas like Coole Park, which have mature woodland on good soils.

(13) Fulacht fia

The low U-shaped mound by the drystone wall is known as a *fulacht fia* or burnt mound. *Fulacht fia* may be translated as 'the cooking place of the deer'. These monuments mainly date from the Bronze Age when it was customary to dig a cavity in the ground and put an oak trough therein. *Fulachtaí fia* are always located near a ready supply of water – in this case the Coole River. The trough was filled with water. Rocks were heated and thrown into the trough. Up to 450 litres of water could be boiled in half an hour using this hot-rock technique. The boiling water could then be used to cook meat, waterproof garments, cure animal skins and to make soap with ash wood and animal skins. *Fulachtaí fia* were also believed to have been used for bathing and hot-rock beer brewing! Their versatility has led to them being described as the Bronze Age equivalent of today's kitchen sink. After repeated use the rocks became so fragmented that they were discarded in the area in front of the trough and thus formed the distinctive horseshoe-shaped mounds we see today.

(14) Hazel

This area is known as Coill na gCnó ('the nut wood'). Hazel is the dominant tree species here. As one of the red squirrel's favourite foodstuffs is the hazelnut, which is abundant here in autumn, it is no surprise that Coill na gCnó is one of the bastions of the red squirrel in the park.

Hazel is found in limestone areas of Ireland often in association with ash. Its leaf litter thickens the soil and thus enables ash to establish itself and eventually become the canopy. Hazel woodlands in the west of Ireland are very humid due to the high rainfall levels and are important habitats for some rare lichens and mosses.

(15) Birds of the Turlough

There is a bird-watching hide to the left of this stop. This is one of the best bird-spotting points in Coole Park as it looks out upon the confluence of the Coole River and the turlough. Mute swans and whooper swans can both be seen here as well as waders such as lapwings and curlews. Ducks include wigeon, teal, pochard and mallard. Other waders occasionally sighted here are redshank, dunlin and golden plover.

Whooper swans are winter visitors taking advantage of the ice-free feeding possiblities in our freshwaters.

(16) The Stone Seat

The limestone seat was built in 1908. It faces eastwards to Lady Gregory's ancestral home at the estate of Roxborough near Loughrea. She spent many hours seated here in the company of her east Galway neighbours, William Butler Yeats and Edward Martyn. Yeats lived nearby at Thoor Ballylee from 1921 to 1929.

(17) The Rich Acre

Sir William Gregory created a woodland of exotic conifers here, in the middle of the nineteenth century. In doing so he displayed the classic Victorian gusto for the novel and the exotic. The Western red cedar, California redwood and Monterey pine evoke western North America more than the west of Ireland. This area of Coill na gCnó is known as 'The Rich Acre', as only the moneyed could afford such an exotic plantation.

We now come to the walled garden, the site of Coole House and the deer pen all of which have been described at stops in the description of the Family Trail above. The last stop is the Deer Pen. As you face the pen, the visitor centre is about 25m to your left along the path.

Lough Avalla Organic Farm – Purple Trail

'He enters into death yearly, and comes back rejoicing. He has seen the light lie down in the dung heap, and rise again in the corn'.
Wendell Berry, 'The Man Born to Farming' (1970).

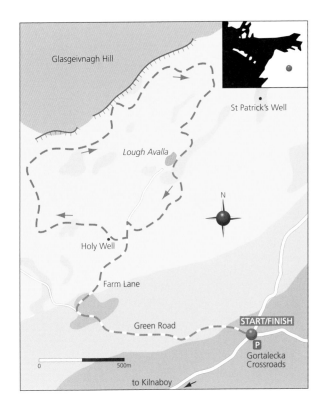

Start/finish: Coming from Corrofin, take the R476 in the direction of Kilfenora and Lisdoonvarna. Drive 3km from Corrofin until you reach the village of Kilnaboy. Take the right turn onto the L1112 opposite Kilnaboy's former post office. Drive 5km until you reach a crossroads. Park at the lay-by on the right just before the crossroads. A display panel at the lay-by contains information regarding the natural heritage of the area.

Description: A looped, waymarked trail. Unsurfaced road, worn paths, farm tracks, some rugged terrain.

Highlights: An uncommon breed of cattle (Belted Galloway), ancient field systems, a prehistoric cairn, limestone pavement, wildflowers, sweeping views into east Clare and north Tipperary and the shores of a small lake, Lough Avalla.

Distance: 6 km (3.7 miles)

Time: 3 hours

Grade: Moderate

Map: *The Burren – a map of the uplands of northwest Clare.* Folding Landscapes. 1:31,680 or OSI *Discovery Series* Map No. 51. Scale: 1:50,000.

(1) Go to Gortlecka crossroads, just a few metres from the lay-by, and turn left onto an unsurfaced road. Thirteen hectares of the rocky land to your right are grazed in winter by cattle as part of the Burren Farming for Conservation programme. The livestock clearly do not have enough grass to survive but their diet is supplemented by other fodder, including nuts. In the past breeds native to Ireland and Britain, such as shorthorns or Aberdeen Angus, would have been the favoured cattle in the Burren. However, market forces have meant that the majority of cattle in the region are now continental breeds such as Charolais and Limousin.

(2) About 1km from the crossroads, you come to a junction. Turn right into Lough Avalla Farm lane. After about 400m, you pass a large open pen for goats. Goat and sheep rearing were widespread in the Burren in the nineteenth century. Latterly, however, cattle production has been dominant. In fact, there may be as few as ten goat farmers left in the entire region. Kid goat meat, known in Irish as *mionán*, was a great spring dish in the Burren in the past. The goats here are raised for both meat and excellent farmhouse cheese.

(3) Turn left as indicated just after the pen. You have now stepped on to the Lough Avalla farm. You will soon come to a haven on the left of the trail with spring water gushing out of the rock. The spring is believed by some to be

a holy well, although it is debatable whether or not the spring was venerated in the past. Be that as it may, the site is visited by some who believe in the therapeutic value of the water. There is a *fulacht fia* within a few metres of the spring. Nearby are stone structures (minus roofs) which functioned as sweat lodges in the past. The sweat houses, where

Site of spring and fulacht fia.

people rid their bodies of toxins, would have used boiling water from the *fulacht fia*.

(4) You reach a spectacular rising platform of limestone pavement. The words 'crazy pavement' come readily to mind. Limestone pavement is rare and precious internationally and the Burren is the most extensive limestone pavement region in Europe. The stone is known locally as the 'warm stone' as it absorbs heat in spring/summer and releases it in autumn/winter. The bedrock for 50 per cent of Ireland is limestone but only in the Burren and a very small number of other localities in the country has the soil been removed and the bedrock exposed. Cross the pavement, walk across a field and you soon pass a tall drystone structure. It is quite a recent construction and not to be confused with archaeological monuments.

(5) Veer right and walk alongside the steep cliffs on your left. The classic topography of the Burren hills is terrace and cliff. Horizontal lines of weakness in the rock were eroded by water. The loosened rock was removed by glaciers, leaving this distinctive stepped landform. The steep cliffs are part of Glasgeivnagh Hill, the summit of which is a plateau with a dense concentration of cairns.

With your back to the cliffs, the views are breathtaking. The Slieve Bernagh range is to the southeast near the village of Killaloe. Beyond this range lies the Slieve Felim range, which straddles parts of Counties Limerick and Tipperary.

(6) Having walked less than a kilometre along the cliff face, you begin the descent through scrub and pasture. Cattle, sheep and goats are raised on the farm. Farming in Ireland has largely become much more specific and intense in the last three decades as it has been transformed by subsidy-driven EU farm policy. However, this holding remains a steadfastly traditional Irish farm with an eclectic range of activities and produce. Moreover, the traditional low-intensity farming regime means that the

A young trekker negotiates the crazy pavement.

holding is very rich in biodiversity. The result on this farm is sublime beef, lamb, kid goat meat and goat's cheese products.

(7) When crossing a rocky, rugged stretch of the trail, look both left and right to see rows of unusually small fields of indeterminate age. These fields are a joy to behold as they remind one of the traditional Irish field type prior to the modernisation of farming. There is a steep drop where a wooden bannister has been added to aid the descent. This area is known as 'the staircase'.

(8) You will pass through some sublime Atlantic hazel woodland with a floor rich in primitive plant communities. Having descended for about a kilometre, you approach the shores of Lough Avalla. The small lake is very deep – up to 30m. Vegetation has colonised a large part of the former surface of the lake. Lough Avalla has long been home to eels and sticklebacks, which have been joined recently by introduced trout and perch. Walk around the lake, pass the jetty and then turn left as indicated.

(9) The path goes uphill a little to where you can enjoy one last glimpse of the farmstead. There are very few looped walking trails in Ireland situated on working farms. This trail is all the more special as the farm through which it passes is organic, part of the paltry 1.2 per cent of the land that is organically farmed. Ireland is nearly bottom of the EU league for organic farming.

(10) You reach the farm lane again. Walk along it till you meet the unsurfaced road. Turn left here. The unsurfaced road leads you back to Gortlecka crossroads. Turn right at the crossroads. The trailhead and lay-by is on your left-hand side.

Árainn: East of Island

'The island has the character and personality of a mute God ... Over it broods an overwhelming sense of great, noble tragedy.'
Liam O'Flaherty, in a letter to his publisher (1927)

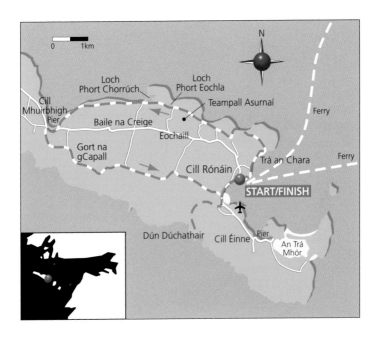

Start/finish: Ferry services to the island operate from Doolin, County Clare, in spring and summer. They operate from Rossaveel, County Galway, all year round. The walk starts at the main island pier in Cill Rónáin.

Description: A long but inspiring walk on minor roads and tracks with a steep climb and some uneven terrain. The walk forms part of the waymarked trail, the Inis Mór Way.

Highlights: Great coastal views, seal viewing, wetland birds, Early Christian sites, cliff forts and a rich range of wildflowers.

Distance 21km (13 miles)

Time: 6.5 hours

Grade: Moderate to strenuous

Map: *Oileáin Arann. A Map of the Aran Islands, County Galway.* Folding Landscapes. Scale: 1:28,160 or OSI *Oileáin Arann, The Aran Islands.* Scale: 1:25,000.

(1) Walk the short distance from the pier to a T-junction. The bustling village of Cill Rónáin ('Ronan's chapel') is to your left. You turn right, however, onto the coast road heading north, which passes two beaches – one of shingle and one of sand. The first beach is Trá na bhFrancach ('the beach of the French') and the second is Trá an Chara ('the beach of the ford'). Turn left onto the lane at the end of Trá an Chara. Loch an Chara ('the lake of the ford') is the lake on the left as you stroll down this short lane. Liam Lysaght's *Atlas of the Breeding Birds of the Burren and the Aran Islands* (2002) estimates that there are sixty breeding bird species on the Aran Islands. Loch an Chara is a delightful spot for some 'birding'. Waders here include sandpipers, whimbrels, turnstones and lapwings. (2) The lane goes around the west of the lake. The first lane on the right at the west of the lake takes you to the sandy beach of Trá na Muailte ('the beach of the hillocks'). The south Connemara coastline is on the opposite side of Galway Bay. A lane on the west

There has been a serious decline in the population of breeding curlews in Ireland over the last three decades.

of the beach will bring you to a junction of the road, which connects the villages of Cill Rónáin and Cill Mhuirbhigh ('chapel on the sandy land'). Turn right at the junction heading towards Cill Mhuirbhigh. The 'green land' in this area makes for good summer pasture for the cattle.

(3) Walk 1km from the junction to arrive at a lane on the left of the road. The signpost indicates the short ascent to Teampall Chiaráin ('St Ciarán's chapel'). This Early Christian site also contains an oratory, sundial, holy well and a number of cross-decorated pillars. The pillars probably served as grave markers though they may also have had other functions.

(4) You will see a stone water-collector built up against a drystone wall on the left, 100m before the turn for the next ecclesiastical site, Teampall Asurnaí ('St Sourney's chapel'). The collectors trap rainwater and recycle it as drinking water for the cattle. There are hundreds of these water-collectors on the Aran Islands, and most date to the early twentieth century as they were subsidised by the Congested Districts Board. The Board's function was to address problems of underdevelopment in the west of Ireland.

Another interesting feature along this drystone wall is a *bearna* (from Irish, literally 'gap', but used on the Aran Islands to mean 'stone gate'), which is used to control the movement of livestock. These stone gates are often imperceptible to the untrained eye. However, the distinguishing feature is stones that are whitened at the edges as they are dismantled and rebuilt on each occasion the cattle enter or leave the field. The gates are an ingenious response to the historical lack of wood on the island. They are about a metre wide and have recently been replaced in a lot of cases by metal gates under the Rural Environmental Protection Scheme (REPS).

A stone gate on the Aran Islands, known locally as a bearna (gap).

(5) Teampall Asurnaí is also a signposted, short climb up a lane to the left of the road. It contains a small, roofless chapel and some ancient graves. You pass the island's recycling centre 100m after the turn for Asurnaí.

Baile Eochla ('Eochaill's village') is on high ground to your left. The most prominent structures in the village are Dún Eochla ('Eochaill's fort') and a signal tower. Dún Eochla is a great, two-walled early medieval fort whilst the signal tower is one of many such coastal defences built by the British authorities in the early 1800s.

(6) Loch Phort Eochla ('the lake at Eochaill's harbour') is a small turlough in a field to the right. A drystone wall runs through the turlough area – proof that this is a highly fluctuating environment. In very wet spells, the loch becomes a wetland habitat while in dry weather it can be an excellent grazing field for cattle. The wall is patched with a colourful coastal lichen called yellow scales, which is found on rocks and walls near the sea.

(7) Loch Phort Chorrúch ('the lake of the bent creek') is a lake to the right just beyond the turlough. Whooper swans are winter visitors from Iceland as they have ice-free feeding opportunities here that are lacking at home. The lake is also home to curlews and waders. Pass the former seaweed factory, the Marine Salts Company, on your left. Seaweed was burned here to make kelp in Victorian times. Kelp is a source of various salts but it was also sold on the mainland by islanders for the making of soap, glass and chemicals.

(8) Port Chorrúch ('bent-creek harbour') is just below the factory and it is the island's most popular weed shore. A large network of lanes crosses the island to ensure that most of the islanders have access to the shores in order to collect seaweed. As soil was so scarce, land-hungry islanders 'made land' for vegetable/potato growing through an amalgamation of seaweed, sand and animal manure. Some islanders still collect seaweed as fertiliser for their potato plots.

(9) A seal-viewing point with an information display board has been created in a lay-by overlooking Port Chorrúch. There are two species of seal off Ireland's shores: the grey seal and the common/harbour seal. Both species can be seen here. At low tide the seals can be seen on the rocks. At high tide they are 'gone fishing'. Pollack, salmon and rockfish are the most common prey of the seals in this area.

(10) As you continue west along the road, Connemara's great mountain ranges are across Galway Bay to the north. The island's western settlements of Cill Mhuirbhigh (left) and Sruthán (right) are straight ahead of you in the distance. About 3km beyond the kelp factory, thousands of large, rounded stones rise from the shore to the level of the road. This steep landform of sand, gravel and rounded stones was thrown up onto the shore by storms and is known as a storm beach. The rounded stones are used in the making of some of the drystone walls (known as storm-beach walls) around the foreshores of the islands. A popular summer bathing beach

is located at Port Mhuirbhigh ('sandy land harbour'), just beyond the storm beach. Walk along the track above the beach until you reach a well-signposted junction.

(The visit to the great prehistoric cliff fort of Dún Aonghasa is included in Route 15, p. 99, and is described at point (1) therein. However, if you wish to visit the fort as part of this walk, go straight through this junction for 200m and then turn left to arrive in the village of Cill Mhuirbhigh. The fort is signposted at the entrance of a laneway ahead of you. There is a short, steep climb to the fort. Allow about an hour for the visit to Dún Aonghasa.)

(11) Turn left at this junction and stroll on for 750m. Take the right turn at the junction at this point and start heading south for the village of Gort na gCapall ('the field of the horses'), the birthplace of the writer Liam O'Flaherty (1896–1984). He was a short-story writer, novelist and communist. His novel *The Informer* was filmed by John Ford in the USA. O'Flaherty's finest novel was *The Famine* written in 1937. A small, commemorative garden in his honour is located in the village.

Goats are used as landscape managers on the Aran Islands as they browse unwanted scrub.

An erratic on the Aran Islands. The granite boulder was conveyed here from south Connemara by glacial action.

(12) Walk straight through the village in an easterly direction and continue along a surfaced road which eventually peters out. You now begin walking along a rough track, which becomes quite steep. The ascent takes you to some of the highest points on the island. At a junction 1.5km from the village, you may exercise the option of turning left down a track to visit Teampall an Ceathrar Álainn ('the church of the four beauties') and its holy well and then retrace your steps to the junction to continue our walk along the Inis Mór Way.

(13) This leg of the Inis Mór Way offers great views of the island. Dún Aonghasa can be seen to the west. There are also fine close-up views of the island's hundreds of tiny fields. Cattle are transferred to these southern and the

southwestern parts of Árainn in winter in the local version of transhumance. The winter grazing lands are easily identifiable thanks to the substantial drystone walls and *botháin* or stone huts. The supplementary winter fodder (principally hay) is stored in the *botháin*. By grazing these lands in winter only, the cattle fulfil a critical ecological role. They manage the landscape well as they prevent the growth of vigorous grasses and scrub which would otherwise outcompete the delicate wildflowers.

If you have the good fortune to walk this trail in spring and summer, some of the floral highlights are spring gentian and several orchid species, such as early-purple orchid, pyramidal orchid, common spotted-orchid and Irish or dense-flowered orchid. The Irish or dense-flowered orchid is one of Ireland's few Lusitanian wildflowers, i.e. Mediterranean flora which is also native to Ireland but absent from Great Britain. Most of the south and southwest of the island is designated as a Special Area of Conservation (SAC). An SAC is a prime flora and/or fauna habitat which is afforded protection in law as it is considered to be important on a European as well as an Irish level. The SACs in Inis Meáin and Inis Oírr also broadly correspond to the southern and southwestern parts of those islands.

(14) The descent starts about 1.5km after the signposted turn for Teampall an Ceathrar Álainn. The rough track gives way to surfaced road. Continue walking east until you come to the sea. It is a left turn for Cill Rónáin at the T-junction here. However, you turn right and walk south for 200m until you reach a lane on your right with a signpost indicating Dún Dúchathair ('the black fort'). Take the short stroll into the fort. Dún Dúchathair is yet another strong medieval statement in stone in a spectacular setting. A curious feature is the upright stones placed outside the fort's huge wall as an extra defensive measure. The uprights are known as *chevaux-de-frise* (literally 'Frisian horse').

Fulmars, kittiwakes, razorbills and guillemots all breed on the cliff ledges in the south of the island. Dún Dúchathair is visited by far fewer people than Dún Aonghasa so you may find yourself with only these sea birds for company at the dimming of the day.

It is a 2km trek from the fort to the start/finish point of the walk at Cill Rónáin.

Árainn: West of Island

*Currach lán éisc
Ag teacht chun cladaigh
Ar órmhuir mhall.*

*(A currach full of fish
Approaching the shore
On a slow gold sea.)*

Máirtín Ó Direáin, 'An tEarrach Thiar' (1949)

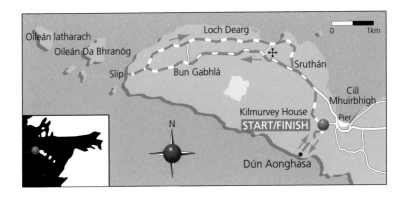

Start/finish: Ferry services to the island operate from Doolin, County Clare, in spring and summer. They operate from Rossaveel, County Galway, all year round. The start/finish point of this walk is at the Dún Aonghasa visitor centre in the middle of the island. You can reach the centre from the main pier at Cill Rónáin by availing of one of the many hackney mini-buses stationed at the pier. An alternative is to hire a bicycle at Cill Rónáin and cycle to the start point. There are bicycle parking facilities at the visitor centre and you may return the bicycle to the bike hire shop after the walk.

Description: A walk along level gradient except for the short, steep ascent to Dún Aonghasa. The walk takes place along minor roads and tracks and is part of the waymarked trail, the Inis Mór way.

Highlights: The spectacular cliff fort of Dún Aonghasa, the extensive ecclesiastical ruins of Na Seacht dTeampaill ('the seven churches'), extensive areas of limestone pavement, Aran wildflowers and magnificent coastal vistas of Galway Bay, Connemara and Black Head in the north of the Burren.

Distance 16km (10 miles)

Time: 5 hours

Grade: Moderate

Map: *Oileáin Arann. A Map of the Aran Islands, County Galway.* Folding Landscapes. Scale: 1:28,160 or OSI *Oileáin Arainn, The Aran Islands.* Scale: 1:25,000.

(1) The Dún Aonghasa visitor centre is at the end of a lane in the village of Cill Mhuirbhigh. The cafe opposite the centre has an open fire and serves good home-made soups.

Dún Aonghasa is a very impressive fort. It has three great defensive walls and is located on a cliff edge with a sheer 80m drop into the Atlantic Ocean. The ascent to the monument from the visitor centre takes about ten minutes. There is a nominal entrance charge and the monument is sensitively managed by the Office of Public Works. Although it was remodelled to a large extent in the medieval period, Dún Aonghasa is the only one of the seven great forts of the Aran Islands to have been built in the Bronze Age.

(2) On leaving the visitor centre, take the first turn left after Kilmurvey House to enter the village of Cill Mhuirbhigh. Veer right around the corner in the village and go to the next junction. There is a disused hostel on your left-hand side. The lane opposite you leads to an excellently preserved beehive hut, Clochán na Carraige ('the

Seaweed drying on an Aran drystone wall.

stone hut of the rock'). Beehive huts served as temporary accommodation for pilgrims visiting the great Christian sites on the western seaboard and the offshore islands. Turn left at the junction and stroll along the main road leading to the west of the island.

Feral goats often browse in the fields to the left. Some farmers use the goats as 'landscape managers' by binding their feet and so confining them to specific areas. The goats thus browse briars that would otherwise encroach upon valuable grasslands. It is a very effective exercise in targeted scrub removal. You will also occasionally spot horses grazing in the fields. They are bred to serve the horse-and-carriage sector of the tourist industry.
(3) The first string of houses along this road forms the village of Sruthán ('the stream'), the birthplace of the poet Máirtín Ó Díreáin (1910–1988), who was one of the finest Irish-language poets of the twentieth century.

Go through the village. You will come to a junction just after the village with a signpost indicating right and seaward for Na Seacht

Black Head. Emma Glanville

dTeampaill ('the seven churches'). Na Seacht dTeampaill is an Early Christian site and home to Teampall Bhreacan ('St Brecan's chapel') and three twelfth-century high crosses. There are also four slabs decorated with crosses in the southeastern corner of the site. The most cryptic of the slabs reads 'VII ROMANI'. Many interesting theories and arguments have been put forward to explain the inscription: my favourite is that the slab commemorates the visit of pilgrims from Rome to Na Seacht dTeampaill in medieval times when the site would have been one of the most westerly outposts of Christendom. Most of the Early Christian sites on the Aran Islands, including Na Seacht dTeampaill, were important destinations for pilgrims in medieval times.

(4) Continue west along the road. A pair of nineteenth-century funerary monuments will catch your eye on the left. The wording on the cenotaphs contains a request for mercy for the deceased. Such monuments are rare in Ireland and there are none at all on either Inis Oírr or Inis Meáin. Pass through Bun Gabhla ('foot of the fork'), the island's most westerly village. Continue west until you arrive at the shore. You have now reached the most westerly point of the Aran Islands.

There are two rock outcrops in front of you: Oileán Dá Bhranóg (Brannock Island) is the nearest rock to the shore; the other is Oileán Iatharach ('the western island') and has an automated lighthouse. The Connemara highlands are to the north whilst the great mass of the Atlantic Ocean lies beyond the outcrops. There is a powerful sense of isolation in this far-flung corner of the island. The slipway is a recent addition and makes life a little easier for the lobster fishermen. Some of the fishermen still go to

sea in currachs, the traditional boat of Ireland's west coast. Currachs featured in Robert Flaherty's famous documentary *Man of Aran* (1934).

(5) Turn around and retrace your steps for half a kilometre. A yellow man painted on a drystone wall will indicate left at this point. The next 4km is along a rough track.

The currach has a light wooden frame over which canvas is stretched. In the past, animal skins were used.

You are now heading eastwards. The famous 'crazy pavements' (limestone pavement) of the Aran Islands are to your left as you progress. The area is alive with colour in spring and summer as flowers and shrubs such as hoary rockrose, bloody crane's-bill, wild thyme, harebell, honeysuckle and burnet rose come into bloom. Hoary rockrose is a rare wildflower in Britain and may be found only on the pavements of the Burren and Árainn in Ireland.

(6) Continue walking in an easterly direction along the track for 3km until you see Loch Dearg ('the red lake') on your left. Loch Dearg is a saltwater lake separated from the sea by a band of shingle. You will then pass a football field on your right. Turn right at the second lane after the football pitch in order to make the modest climb back to Sruthán. Turn left when you reach the road and walk 1.5km to one of the main junctions on the island.

(7) Turn right at the junction and then take the first turn left to return to the village of Cill Mhuirbhigh. Walk down the short lane in the village in order to return to the visitor centre and so complete your loop of the west of the island.

Inis Oírr

*'A dream of limestone in sea light
Where gulls have placed their perfect prints.'*
Derek Mahon, 'Thinking of Inis Oírr in Cambridge, Mass.' (1979)

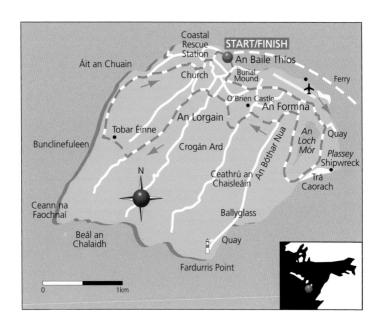

Start/finish: Ferry services to the island operate from Doolin, County Clare, in spring and summer. They operate from Rossaveel, County Galway all year round. The walk starts at Inis Oírr's principal pier.

Description: The waymarked walk, Inis Oírr Way, follows very quiet roads and tracks. The Way is essentially two loops covering the northwest and northeast of the island with some spectacular coastal walking. The description below also includes options to increase the walk distance by up to 4.5km.

Highlights: Wildflowers, coastal birds, magnificent stone walls and a shipwreck.

Distance: 10.5km, not including options (6.5 miles)

Time: 3 to 3.5 hours

Grade: Moderate

Map: *Oileáin Arann. A Map of the Aran Islands, County Galway.* Folding Landscapes, Scale: 1:28,160 or OSI *Oileáin Arainn, The Aran Islands.* Scale: 1:25,000.

(1) The walk starts at the pier at An Baile Thíos. On leaving the pier, take the left turn along the road, which veers right after just 200m. You reach a junction after another 150m. The flat-topped oval mound here is a national monument known as Cnoc Raithní ('hill of bracken'), a Bronze Age burial mound. The smaller round mound on top of the original may have been superimposed in medieval times for the same funerary function.

(2) Turn left at this junction. The Gaelic football pitch and the children's playground are on the right and the island camping facility is on the left. The O'Brien medieval castle is in the eyeline above the football field.

(3) Precisely 400m from the junction you will arrive at a sandy little hill upon which Teampall Chaomháin ('St Caomhán's chapel') is situated. The chapel's nave is the oldest part of the building and dates to approximately 1,000 years ago. The wonder of this roofless structure is enhanced by the fact that it is partially buried in sand. You may exit the chapel/graveyard by the gate on the eastern part of the site.

The grassland immediately outside the gate supports a myriad of lime-loving plants, including autumn lady's tresses in late summer. It is a delicate, small, white orchid with, as its name suggests, a twist in its flowering spike.

(4) Turn left on exiting and descend 100m to the T-junction and turn right. There is a group of three thatched cottages on your right-hand side – a

The Plassey *shipwreck on Inis Oírr features in the opening credits of* Father Ted, *the ecclesiastical comedy series.*

reminder of the vernacular dwellings in which most islanders lived well into the twentieth century. The island airstrip is on the left.

The island's biggest lake, Loch Mór ('the big lake'), comes into view 300m along this road on the right. The lake is a mix of fresh water and seawater and is an important habitat for wildfowl. Mute swans nest on the lake margins. The lake also supports a healthy population of eels. You are now circling the lake in a clockwise direction. As you proceed down this eastern side of the lake, keep an eye out for an Ordnance Survey drystone column on the left. These columns were built as vantage points on which Victorian soldiers perched as they mapped the country.

(5) The *Plassey* shipwreck is on your left and is well worth the 200m detour. Irish saxifrage abounds on the landward side of the wreck, in clumps like small green hedgehogs. This ship ran aground in the 1960s in a violent storm. The sailors all survived, thanks, in part, to the heroism of the local people. The *Plassey* featured famously in the opening reels of the hugely successful TV comedy series, *Father Ted*. You can also enjoy a fine vista of the Cliffs of Moher off to the southeast across the South Sound from the *Plassey*.

(6) It is a 700m walk from the shipwreck to the point where the road starts to veer inland. The road verges along this stretch boast a rich melange of wildflowers, including honeysuckle, harebell, the pyramidal orchid, wild carrot, Irish saxifrage, yarrow and our toxic yellow friend, ragwort, to name just a few. Do also keep an eye out for coastal birds such as sandwich terns, guillemots and Manx shearwater on this stretch between lake and sea.

OPTION: You now have the option of continuing for 1.2km south along a stony beach to the South Aran Lighthouse. If you take this option, you can then return from the lighthouse to the Inis Oírr Way via An Bóthar Nua, 'the new road'. This road runs from the lighthouse in the southeastern extremity of the island to the village of An Formna ('ridge of the hill') in the northeast of the island. The 37m-high lighthouse dominates the skyline in the south of the island. It was built in the mid-1800s and was automated in 1978. Its light can illuminate the seas around to a range of 20 nautical miles. This magnificent detour will add 2.5km to your trek.

(7) The road and the Inis Oírr Way both veer inland at this point. There is a very regular system of small fields to your right as you make a small climb along the road. The drystone walls on these road margins are up to 3m in height – noticeably taller than their counterparts in the Burren, County Clare.

You are now walking northwards along An Bóthar Thoir ('the eastern road'). Loch Mór is to the right. There are magnificent examples of man-made limestone platforms to your left, used for drying seaweed. Leaving the lake behind, you arrive at the most easterly village on the island, An Formna. The village now largely consists of a low-density settlement of late twentieth-century houses, although some ruins of earlier dwellings built from local limestone are evident. Some of the houses have fine views not only of the lake but also of County Kerry off to the southeast (weather permitting, of course).

(8) The road veers left in the village and then heads south along An Bóthar Nua. The island is divided into four *ceathrú* (districts). You are now leaving Ceathrú an Locha ('the lake district') for Ceathrú an Chaisleáin ('the castle district'). There are hundreds of little roads (*bóithríní*) on the island and, in this area, they are aflame with brilliant red and orange colours in summer and autumn as the garden escapees fuchsia and montbretia are in bloom.

Walk along An Bóthar Nua for just 200m until you reach a track on the right. Facing the track, you can admire two highly impressive defensive structures from different periods: a medieval castle on the right and an early nineteenth-century signal tower on the left. Walk 300m to the end of this track, which brings you out onto Bóthar an Chaisleáin ('the castle road').

(9) Turn right here and walk less than 100m to the medieval O'Brien castle on your left-hand side, which is well worth this slight detour. The O'Briens reigned in the kingdom of Thomond in medieval times. Their lifestyle was based on farming and the extended clan. The kingdom included the Aran Islands. The castle was built within an earlier oval stone fort, Dún Formna ('the hilltop fort'). There are just two O'Brien castles on the Aran Islands. The other one is to be found on Árainn. Some archaeologists argue that these

A carved stone head on the O'Brien Castle, Inis Oírr.

two castles and the earlier island forts were built in part as command centres for the important sea trading routes in the vicinity. See if you can find the stone faces on the castle walls.

(10) On leaving the castle, turn right and go back up Bóthar an Chaisleáin for half a kilometre until you reach the grey, rectangular signal tower on the left. The protrusions at the landward side of the tower are machicolations – defensive features through which rocks or burning objects could be dropped on unwanted visitors. You have now reached the highest point of the island at 220m above sea level. The signal towers were built in the early 1800s by the British authorities in Ireland at a time of poor Anglo-French relations. The British feared an invasion of Ireland by French forces sympathetic to the Irish revolutionary cause. The towers accommodated signal and military personnel and acted as a line of communication right across Ireland. These high points of the island afford stunning views of Connemara and its highlands to the north and the rocky Burren to the east.

(11) Just after the signal tower, you will also pass one of the island's water reservoirs on the left. Three hundred metres on from the signal tower, turn right onto a track. This turn will be marked with the yellow waymarked icon of the hiking man. Continue for 100m until you reach a junction. Take the right turn here and continue for another 200 m. At this point, the track merges with a road which veers left for 100 m. Take the right turn here and then the next left at a T-junction. This village is called Baile an Lurgain ('the village of the shaft/shank') and is one of the five villages of the island. Baile an Lurgain and An Baile Thíos ('the lower village') to the west of the pier are the commercial core of the island.

(12) However, our walk now leads us to the splendid serenity of the west of the island. The Coastal Rescue Station is a further 300m ahead on the right-hand side of the road. You are now heading southwards for all of 1.2km along Bóthar an Bhaile Thíos. The road cuts through an enchanting network of small field systems. The field boundaries are all defined by drystone walls. There are estimated to be approximately 2,500km of these walls in total on the three Aran Islands. The stones were removed from the fields in the first instance so that the land could be cultivated. Sand and seaweed were then carried from the shore to form soil. The walls also afford some shelter to the cattle and sheep from the Atlantic rains and

There are approximately 2,500km of drystone walls on the Aran Islands.

gales. Finally, the walls neatly define the landowners' field systems and distinguish their property from their neighbours'. All the walls are, in turn, linear monuments to the Stone Age people who were the pioneer farmers on these islands. After all, it was they who first introduced the concept of drystone walling to the Aran Islands and indeed to Ireland as a whole. (13) This quarter or district of Inis Oírr is known as Ceathrú an Phóilín ('the district of the small hollow'). At the 1.2km mark along this road you will come across another waymarked arrow with its yellow figure. Turn right as indicated on to a track, which is almost 400m in length. Halfway along is the holy well, dedicated to Naomh Éinne (St Enda), proudly signposted in local stone and still frequented by islanders, especially on the saint's feast day. There are estimated to be about 3,000 such holy wells in Ireland and many are still venerated for what is believed to be the curative powers of their sacred waters. Éinne is believed to have been a fifth-century evangelical monk. He is the patron saint of the neighbouring island of Árainn (or Inis Mór – 'big island'). Folk belief has it that an eel occasionally appears in the well. However, only a small number of people have ever had the good fortune to spot it. It is thought to be a highly propitious omen for those who do see it.

The belief that fish are sacred and have supernatural powers is prevalent in many different cultures. This animism is one of the many indicators of the pagan origins of these Christianised sites.
(14) On leaving the holy well, continue 200m along the track to reach the junction with the most westerly road on the island.

OPTION: you may turn left here and walk the extra kilometre to the southwesterly corner of the island. The walk is partly along track and partly along stone beach. This magical, isolated corner is known as Ceann na Faochnaí ('the head of the winkles'), and the swells on the sea here are highly regarded by the surfing community. This detour will add 2km to the trek.

If you exclude this option, just turn right at the junction between track and road. You are now making the final leg of your trek back to the comparative hustle and bustle of An Baile Thíos and Baile An Lurgain. Inis Meáin ('middle island') is on your left and the waters between the two islands are known as An Sunda Salach ('Foul Sound') on account of the rocky ocean bed. A conspicuous feature to your left is the electricity-generating windmills of Inis Meáin, located in the isolated southern extremities of that neighbouring island.

(15) As you make the homeward journey, most of the land between you and the sea is a storm beach with its distinctive rounded stones. A storm beach is one which has been affected by particularly fierce waves. The resultant landform is a steep beach composed of large, rounded stones, shingle and sometimes sand. There are inland cliffs to your right where the most eye-catching wildflower is sea pink or thrift. You may see seaweeds draped over the walls to dry in this area. The dried algae are used as a most ecological fertiliser for potatoes. They can also be mixed with sand in order to form a very scarce commodity around these parts, i.e. soil.

(16) Just over 1km on from the holy well, you arrive at a 'V' in the road. Take the right turn here. Some of the best angling the island has to offer is on the shore to your left. Over twenty different species have been caught here, according to Fishery Board records.

(17) You meet with a T-junction after another kilometre. Turn right and walk 100m to the eleventh-century chapel of Naomh Gobnait (St Gobnat), the patron saint of beekeepers who once unleashed her bees on a rustler attempting to steal her cattle. The site also contains three *leachtanna*

Limestone pavement showing the effects of rainwater solution.

(outdoor altars) and two bullauns (basin stones). The latter may have been used as pestles for herb pounding or as holy water fonts.

(18) On leaving St Gobnat's, turn left and proceed the half kilometre to the next T-junction. You have now reached the core of the village of An Baile Thíos. The pier is another couple of hundred metres to your right.

Inis Meáin

*'I seem to enter into the wild pastimes of the cliff,
a companion to the cormorants and the crows.'*
John Millington Synge, 'The Aran Islands' (1907)

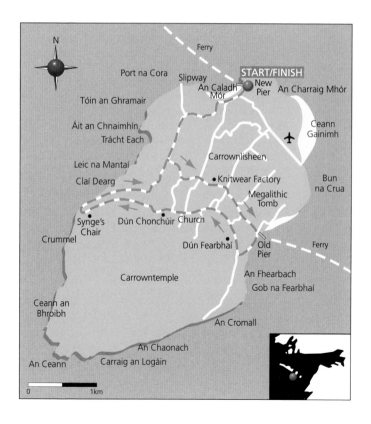

Start/finish: Ferry services to the island operate from Doolin, County Clare, in spring and summer. They operate from Rossaveel, County Galway, all year round. The walk begins and ends at the new pier on the north of the island.

Description: Mostly along the waymarked walk, known as the Inis Meáin Way, is mostly along very quiet, tarred roads and paths with a short section crossing limestone pavement.

Highlights: Two of the seven great stone forts of the Aran Islands and stunning views of the western seaboard to the north and south of Inis Meáin.

Distance: 8km (5 miles)

Time: 2.5 hours

Grade: Casual

Maps: *Oileáin Arann. A Map of the Aran Islands, County Galway.* Folding Landscapes, Scale: 1: 28,160 or OSI *Oileáin Arainn, The Aran Islands.* Scale: 1:25,000.

(1) The new pier, An Caladh Mór (built in 2010), is in the north of the island. When you disembark, go west along the road and take the last turn left. You are now walking south along Bóthar Chinn an Bhaile. When you reach a pair of cylindrical water storage tanks (source of the island's water supply), turn left into Bóithrín an Turlaigh ('the road of the turlough').

(2) Walk along this road for 800m until you reach a four-cross road. Go straight across the junction. The eye-catching building on the terrace up to your right is Inis Meáin restaurant and suites. It blends in well with the topography as it is low-rise and built of limestone. The food is a celebration of island produce, including fish and the flouriest of potatoes. The same family owns the knitwear factory, which you will shortly pass on the left. The knitwear justifiably enjoys an international reputation though the soft fibres are almost all imported.

(3) Turn right at the next T-junction and almost immediately take the next turn left. Walk along this road for 100m. A wonderful detour now offers itself if you turn left here. Pass the first house on your left (a guest house). A bewildering spectacle of exposed limestone pavement will almost immediately greet you in the field to the left of the road. Enter the field by a stile in the wall. The grikes (fissures) were infilled with stones by land-hungry islanders in the past and the pavements were subsequently covered with a topsoil of seaweed and sand. The soil has long since been eroded by human exploitation and the winds. However,

A bothán (shed) on Inis Meáin used for storing hay as winter fodder for the cattle.

the stone-filled grikes are a reminder of how islanders once 'reinvented' this challenging glaciated landscape in order to subsist. There is also a degraded wedge tomb in this field, probably the resting place of the special dead of some of the earliest island farmers from Stone Age times.

(4) Return to the T-junction. Turn left, then take the next turn right. Proceed along the surfaced road and track until you reach Dún Fearbhaí (Fearbha's Fort). The *bóithrín* is a little botanical nirvana. Great willowherb, Babington's leek, bloody crane's-bill, burnet rose, blackthorn, marsh woundwort, alexanders and honeysuckle are just some of the wildflowers and plants which brilliantly colour the track in summer.

Dún Fearbhaí strategically occupies high ground on the east of the island with commanding views of the sea routes off to the west. It is one of seven large stone forts on the Aran Islands and is built in the typical Aran style with terracing and steps inside the enormous walls. The fort was probably inhabited by the political masters of the islands for over a thousand years up to the 1600s.

(5) On returning to the junction of the *bóithrín* and the tarred road, turn left. Take the next left turn just over 100m further on. You are on the principal road of the island, which runs east–west. Pass the island's telephone exchange on your left-hand side. There is a stone shed with a thatched roof opposite the exchange which is used to store winter fodder (hay) for the cattle. These sheds are common on the Aran Islands.

Inis Meáin's only pub is on your right, a mere 250m beyond the exchange, with proudly whitewashed walls and a thatched roof. There is a colourful and immaculately maintained Madonna and Child statue in a limestone grotto on your left 200m beyond the pub. Siopa Ruairí Bhig (Ruairí's shop) is the next landmark. It is on the left and is the main island shop.

Juniper growing on limestone pavement.

Water harvester, Inis Meáin. The design and concept are said to have originated in the Middle East.

(6) The parish priest's house is just before the island's church on the left-hand side of the road. The ruin of the early Christian chapel in the grounds of the priest's house is known as Teampall na Seacht Mac Rí ('the church of the king's seven sons'). The stone cross by the chapel is said to mark the grave of Naomh Cinndhearg (St Cinndhearg). A holy well dedicated to the saint is situated 50m southwest of the ruined church in the next field beyond the priest's back garden.

The contemporary church (1938) houses magnificent stained-glass portraits of Mary Magdalen and Saints Caomhán, Einne (Enda) and Brecan. The saints' portraits are an artistic homage to Ireland's glorious spiritual past. The windows came from the studios of Harry Clarke, the most prolific and influential stained-glass Irish artist of the twentieth century whose work is much admired internationally.

(7) Teach Synge (Synge's House) soon comes into view on the right-hand side of the road. It is a 300-year-old whitewashed thatched cottage. John Millington Synge, the famous dramatist, lived here for several summers at the beginning of the twentieth century. He wrote *The Aran Islands* (1907) in this house, a fascinating document of the three Aran islands and their people in the early 1900s. The house now functions as a museum to the life and writings of Synge which, during the high season, is open daily at lunchtime.

(8) The island's most impressive monument, Dún Chonchúir ('Conor's fort'), is a couple of hundred metres beyond Synge's cottage to the left of the road. Situated in the west of the island, the fort commands impressive views of Connemara and even of Mount Brandon in Kerry to the south. The most westerly protrusion you can see in Connemara is Errisbeg, an isolated hill above the village of Roundstone. Dún Chonchúir has two concentric

stone walls and it is without doubt a sister fort of Dún Feabhraí on the east of the island. The inner walls rise to a height of 6m and are 5m thick in places. In the absence of excavation, the fort is believed to have been the homestead of early medieval chiefs.

(9) On leaving the fort, continue west along the road for 400m until you come to a signpost for a *clochán* (old stone structure). The *clochán* is a very short distance along a path to the left of the road. *Clocháin* are known colloquially as beehive huts on account of their shape. They date to early medieval times and are located at ecclesiastical sites. The western seaboard and offshore islands had many great pilgrimage stations right up to the eleventh and twelfth centuries. The *clocháin* are believed to have been built as lodgings for the pilgrims. Eminent Irish archaeologist Dr Peter Harbison has colourfully described the huts as 'Ireland's first and oldest surviving bed and breakfast establishments'.

(10) You shortly pass the most westerly houses on the island. Eventually, you come to the end of the road and you commence a 100m walk along a worn path in order to reach Cathaoir Synge (Synge's Chair). The 'chair' is, in fact, a drystone wind shelter, constructed long before Synge made it famous. The dramatist spent many summer days perched here, soaking in the breathtaking scenery of neighbouring Inis Mór, Connemara and the Atlantic Ocean, patrolled by black-green shags, stiff-winged fulmars and brilliant white gannets. There are also a few invasive mini-dolmens built by insensitive visitors in evidence hereabouts. Please do not emulate them!

(11) Descend seawards and turn right (east) through the fields and exploit the openings which the drystone walls have to offer. You soon reach one of the island's *bóithríní*. The storm beach down below it is one of the most impressive in Ireland, rising as it does to over 50m above sea level. This area also boasts a wonderful profusion of sea thrift. The knotted pearlwort, with its white petals, is also much in evidence here in late summer.

On the right of the *bóithrín* you may see grazing sheep, with feet bound so that they are constrained to engage in the targeted removal of scrub in a specific area – a practice also used on the Shetland Islands.

Meanwhile, keep an eye along the seaward side for examples of glacial erratics composed of granite. These boulders were deposited here by glaciers towards the end of the last Ice Age. The erratics originated in the granite regions of south Connemara.

Sea ivory is one of several lichens which thrives on the erratics. It is tufted and has a beautiful, silvery green colour. The lichen is known in Irish as *Féasóg na gCreag* ('the beard of the rock').

(12) The *bóithrín* merges with one of the principal roads of the island, Bóthar Chinn an Bhaile. Turn left at this junction and walk 1km more northwards along this road to return to the pier.

Glossary

Boulder Clay	an amalgam of rock, soil and clay debris deposited by glaciers during the Ice Age.
Cist	a small, prehistoric burial chamber made from stone.
Clint	blocks making up part of limestone pavement, separated by grikes, or fissures.
Drumlin	a low, oval hill consisting of compacted boulder clay – a glacial landform.
Erratic	a boulder brought from a distance by glaciers.
Fulacht Fia	a Bronze Age monument also known as a 'burnt mound'. May have had several different functions including use as an outdoor cooking site or as a bathing pit/steam bath.
Grike	a fissure separating blocks (clints) of limestone pavement.
Karst	a landscape of highly soluble rock, which has been eroded by rainwater to produce distinct landforms.
Polje	a flat-floored depression hollowed out by the dissolution of rock by rainwater (from Serbo-Croat).
Swallow hole	a cavity in the ground caused by water solution.
Turlough	a seasonal lake of limestone regions in the west of Ireland. When the underground water level rises, groundwater may appear temporarily in the form of a turlough.

A sheep's pass in a drystone wall. One of many vernacular structures to be found on Burren farms.

Latin Names

Alexanders	*Smyrnium olusatrum*
ash	*Fraxinus excelsior*
autumn lady's tresses	*Spiranthes spiralis*
Babington's leek	*Allium babingtonii*
beech	*Fagus sylvatica*
bee orchid	*Ophrys apifera*
bell heather	*Erica cinerea*
bird's-nest orchid	*Neottia nidus-avis*
blackthorn	*Prunus spinosa*
bloody crane's-bill	*Geranium sanguineum*
bluebell	*Hyacinthoides non-scripta*
bird's-foot trefoil	*Lotus corniculatus*
black bog-rush	*Schoenus nigricans*
blackthorn	Prunus spinosa
blue moor-grass	*Sesleria caerulea*
bog asphodel	*Narthecium ossifragum*
bog myrtle	*Myrica gale*
box	*Buxus sempervivens*
bracken	*Pteridium aquilinum*
bramble	*Rubus fruticosus*
broad-leaved helleborine	*Epipactis helleborine*
burnet rose	*Rosa pimpenellifolia*
California redwood	*Sequoia sempervirens*
carline thistle	*Carlina vulgaris*
cherry laurel	*Prunus laurocerasus*
common butterwort	*Pinguicula vulgaris*
cotton grass	*Eriophorum angustifolium*
common gorse	*Ulex europaeus*
common milkwort	*Polygala vulgaris*
common snowberry	*Symphoricarpos albus*
common spotted-orchid	*Dactylorhiza fuchsii*
cowslip	*Primula veris*
deer grass	*Trichophorum cespitosum*
devil's-bit scabious	*Succisa pratensis*
dog rose	*Rosa canina*
early-purple orchid	*Orchis mascula*
false oxlip	*Primula x polyantha*
fen violet	*Viola persicifolia*
fern	*Pteropsida*
flecked marsh-orchid	*Dactylorhiza cruenta*
fly orchid	*Ophrys insectifera*
fragrant orchid	*Gymnadenia conopsea*
fuchsia	*Fuchsia magellanica*
goldenrod	*Solidago virgaurea*
golden-scaled male fern	*Dryopteris affinis*

great willowherb	*Epilobium hirsutum*
guelder-rose	*Viburnum opulus*
harebell	*Campanula rotundifolia*
hare's-tail cotton grass	*Eriopohorum vaginatum*
hart's-tongue fern	*Phyllitis scolopendrium*
hawthorn	*Crataegus monogyna*
hazel	*Corylus avellana*
heath spotted-orchid	*Dactylorhiza maculata*
herb Robert	*Geranium robertianum*
hoary rockrose	*Helianthemum oelandicum*
holly	*Ilex aquifolium*
honeysuckle	*Lonicera periclymenum*
horse chestnut	*Aesculus hippocastanum*
Indian bean tree	*Catalpa bignonioides*
Irish eyebright	*Euphrasia salisburgensis*
Irish or dense-flowered orchid	*Neotinia maculata*
Irish saxifrage	*Saxifraga rosacea*
ivy	*Hedera helix*
juniper	*Juniperis communis*
knapweed	*Centaurea nigra*
knotted pearlwort	*Sagina nodosa*
lesser butterfly orchid	*Platanthera bifolia*
lesser celandine	*Ranunculus ficaria*
lime	*Tilia x europaea*
ling or common heather	*Calluna vulgaris*
lords and ladies	*Arum maculatum*
marsh dandelion	*Taraxacum palustre*
marsh woundwort	*Stachys palustris*
meadowsweet	*Filipendula vulgaris*
montbretia	*Crocosmia x crocosmiiflora*
Monterey pine	*Pinus radiata*
mountain avens	*Dryas octopetala*
mountain everlasting	*Antennaria dioica*
northern bedstraw	*Galium boreale*
Norway spruce	*Picea abies*
pedunculate oak	*Quercus robur*
polypody fern	*Polypodium australe*
primrose	*Primula vulgaris*
purging buckthorn	*Rhamnus carthartica*
purple moor-grass	*Molinia caerulea*
pyramidal bugle	*Ajuga pyramidalis*
pyramidal orchid	*Anacamptis pyramidalis*
ragwort	*Senecio jacobaea*
ramsons	*Allium ursinum*
red valerian	*Centranthus ruber*
rue-leaved saxifrage	*Saxifraga tridactylites*
rusty-back fern	*Ceterach officinarum*
St John's Wort	*Hypericum perforatum*

sanicle	*Sanicula europaea*
Scots pine	*Pinus sylvestris*
sea ivory	*Ramalina siliquosa*
sea pink (or thrift)	*Armeria maritima*
selfheal	*Prunella vulgaris*
sessile oak	*Quercus petraea*
shrubby cinquefoil	*Potentilla fruticosa*
silver birch	*Betula pendula*
soft shield fern	*Polystichum setiferum*
spindle	*Euonymus europaeus*
spring gentian	*Gentiana verna*
sycamore	*Acer pseudoplatanus*
thyme broomrape	*Orobanche alba*
tormentil	*Potentilla erecta*
tutsan	*Hypericum androsaaemum*
western red cedar	*Thuja plicata*
whitethorn	*Crataegus monogyna*
white water lily	*Nymphaea alba*
wild angelica	*Angelica syvlestris*
wild carrot	*Daucus carota*
wild garlic	*Allium ursinum*
wild thyme	*Thymus polytrichus*
willow	*Salix*
Wilson's honeysuckle	*Lonicera nitida*
wood anemone	*Anemone nemorosa*
wood violet	*Viola reichenbachiana*
wood sorrel	*Oxalis acetosella*
yarrow	*Achillea millefolium*
yellow iris	*Iris pseudacorus*
yellow-rattle	*Rhinanthus minor*
yellow scales	*Xanthoria parietina*
yellow-wort	*Blackstonia perfoliata*
yew	*Taxus baccata*

Bibliography

Aalen, F. H. A., Whelan, K. and Stout, M. (eds.) (1997). *Atlas of the Irish Rural Landscape*. Cork University Press.

Balmey, M., Fitter, R. and Fitter, A. (2003). *Wild Flowers of Britain and Ireland*. Domino Guides.

Cunningham, G. (1980). *Burren Journey West*. Shannonside Mid-Western Regional Tourism Organisation.

Cunningham, G. (1992). *Burren Journey North*. Burren Research Press.

Darcy, G. (1992). *A Natural History of the Burren*. Immel Publishing Ltd.

Darcy, G. (2006). *The Burren Wall*. Tír Eolas.

Dempsey, E. and O'Clery, M. (2002). *The Complete Guide to Ireland's Birds 2nd edition*. Gill & Macmillan.

Dunford, B. (2002). *Farming and the Burren*. Teagasc.

Fuller, J. (2007). *Buds of the Banner. A Guide to Growing Native Trees and Shrubs in Clare*. Rural Resource Development Ltd.

Gibbons, B. (2011). *Wildflowers Wonders of the World*. New Holland Publishers.

Hayden, T. and Harrington, R. (2000). *Exploring Irish Mammals*. Townhouse Dublin.

Hickie, D. (2002). *Native Trees and Forests of Ireland*. Gill & Macmillan.

Jones, C. (2004). *The Burren and the Aran Islands*. Exploring the Archaeology. The Collins Press.

Lalor, B. (ed.) (2003). *The Encyclopaedia of Ireland*. Gill & Macmillan.

Lysaght, L. (2002). *An Atlas of the Breeding Birds of the Burren and the Aran Islands*. Birdwatch Ireland.

Mac Coitir, N. (2003). *Irish Trees: Myths, Legends and Folklore*. The Collins Press.

Mac Coitir, N. (2006). *Irish Wild Plants: Myths, Legends and Folklore*. The Collins Press.

MacMahon, M. (2013). *The Parish of Corofin – a historical profile*. Michael MacMahon.

Nelson, E. C. (1997). *The Burren: A Companion to the Wildflowers of an Irish Limestone Wilderness*. Samton Ltd.

Nelson, C. (1999) *Wild Plants of the Burren and the Aran Islands*. The Collins Press.

O'Connell, J. W. and Korff, A. (eds.) (2001). *The Book of the Burren, 2nd Updated Edition*. Tír Eolas.

O'Donovan, J. and Curry, E. (1997). *The Antiquities of County Clare. Ordnance Survey Letters 1839*. Clasp Press.

O'Rourke, C. (2006). *Nature Guide to the Aran Islands*. The Lilliput Press.

O'Sullivan, P. (ed.) (1977). *The Aran Islands: A World of Stone*. O'Brien Press.

O'Sullivan, P. (1995). *Dromore Wood National Nature Reserve. The Castle Trail and the Rabbit Island Trail Walks*. The Office of Public Works.

Pilcher, J. and Hall, V. (2001). *Flora Hibernica. The wildflowers, plants and trees of Ireland*. The Collins Press.

Press, B. and Hosking, D. (1992). *Trees of Britain and Europe. Photographic Field Guide*. New Holland.

Robinson, T. (1996). *Oileáin Árann. A Companion to the Map of the Aran Islands*. Folding Landscapes.

Simms, M. (2001). *Exploring the Limestone Landscapes of the Burren and the Gort Lowlands*. Burrenkarst.com.

Swinfen, A. (1992). *Forgotten Stones, Ancient Church Sites of the Burren and Environs*. The Lilliput Press.

Westropp, T. J. (1999). *Archaeology of the Burren, Prehistoric Forts and Dolmens in North Clare*. Clasp Press.

Acknowledgements

I would like to thank Seán Ó Riain, Stephen Ward (sometime walking companion) and Emma Glanville (National Parks and Wildlife Service) for their valuable advice and support. Gratitude and compliments to Carles Casasin for the striking illustrations. Love and emotion for Eimer and Seanán who allowed me to divide so much time between laptop and limestone. All errors are mine.

Thanks also to the following people for their generous assistance:

Comyn, Bernie and Doreen. Lough Rask, Ballyvaughan.
Connole, Frances and staff. Burren Visitor Centre, Kilfenora.
Costello, Nancy. Ordnance Survey of Ireland.
Krieger, Carsten. Kilbaha.
Faherty, Angela. Inis Meáin.
Fisherman's Cottage. Inis Oírr,
Gleeson, Carol. Burren Connect.
Howard, Mary. Fanore.
Hynes, Paddy. Folklorist. Carran.
Jeuken, Harry. Kilnaboy.
Lawless, Helen. Wicklow Uplands Council.
Mac Donncha, An t-Uasal. Sruthán, Árainn.
McCarthy, Eimer. LEADER.
McCarthy, Jim. Village Stores, Ballyvaughan.
McInerney, Bill. Carran.
McLoughlin, Hilda. NPWS. Coole Park.
McNamara, Maria. Geologist.
McNamara, Pat and Gillian. Fanore.
Meehan, Dr Robert. Consultant geologist, Talamhireland.
Murphy, John. Clare Birdwatching.
O'Rourke, Dr Con. Institute of Biology of Ireland.
Orr, Tim. Mountaineering Council of Ireland.
Pierson, Beverley. Leave No Trace Ireland.
Quilligan, Flann. Shannon Development.
Parr, Dr Sharon. Scientific Co-ordinator, Burren Life Project.
Sheehy-Skeffington, Dr Micheline. Department of Botany. NUI Galway.
Sherlock, Rory. Archaeologist.
Vaughan, Mickey. Burren farmer. Cappanawalla.
Zollinger, Elizabeth. Árainn.